MIDAS
INVESTING

MIDAS
INVESTING

HOW YOU CAN MAKE AT LEAST 20% IN THE STOCK MARKET THIS YEAR AND EVERY YEAR

JONATHAN STEINBERG

TIMES BUSINESS

RANDOM HOUSE

Library of Congress Cataloging-in-Publication Data

Steinberg, Jonathan.
    Midas investing : how you can make at least 20% in the stock
  market this year and every year / Jonathan Steinberg.
      p.   cm.
  Includes bibliographical references and index.
  ISBN 0-8129-2388-X (hardcover)
    1. Stocks. 2. Investments. 3. Stock exchanges—United States.
  I. Title.
  HG4661.S77   1996
  332.63'22—dc20   96-20994

Random House website address: http://www.randomhouse.com/

9 8 7 6 5 4 3 2

First Edition

*This book is dedicated to Abe Herzog
and to the memory of Jules Steinberg.*

Acknowledgments

Success has many fathers, as the saying goes, and the point certainly rings true with the creation of this book. First and foremost, I want to thank Andrew Feinberg for all his help and hard work on this book. Andy is one of America's most respected financial journalists, and his work has appeared in journals too numerous to mention. He is the author of another personal-finance book, *Downsize Your Debt* (Penguin Books: 1993), and is in every way the co-author of *Midas Investing*. Through countless hours of interviews, editing, and writing, Andy performed a yeoman job in bringing this project to fruition. In fact, it is fair to say that without his efforts *Midas Investing* would never have seen the light of day, and I am deeply grateful to him.

I also want to thank Gordon Anderson, who was also instrumental in this book's creation. He has been the editor of *Individual Investor* for more than seven years and has worked hand in hand with me to build the magazine into what I sincerely believe is the finest personal-finance publication in America. Gordon reviewed every word of this book, critiquing my arguments and helping me fine-tune my message.

The rest of the *Individual Investor* team helped me too. Research director Tom Byrne played a key role in helping me to bring dry financial concepts to life. And, of course, he was even more vital in helping pick the top-performing stocks that supply most of the examples in this book. Others on the staff contributed in various important ways. Jonathan Moreland, for his work on insider trading, and momentum-investing expert Lex Haris are worthy of particular note. I also want to thank the rest of the magazine's talented staff for their persistence and perspiration in building *Individual Investor* itself.

Acknowledgments

I also want to acknowledge all the people at Times Books. I owe deep thanks to Karl Weber, who helped us conceive of the book. I'm equally grateful to Geoff Shandler, whose skillful editing was responsible for turning my sometimes rambling commentary into crisp, clean prose.

Last, I want to make a personal note. I have dedicated this book to my grandfathers, Abe Herzog and the late Jules Steinberg. Both of them encouraged me to explore and develop my business and investing skills. They and my grandmothers, Freda Herzog and Ann Steinberg, have given me a lifetime of love and encouragement for which I feel truly blessed. Their support has enabled me to achieve success.

I also want to thank my parents, Barbara Steinberg and Saul Steinberg, for their unconditional love and support. It was my father who most influenced me to undertake this business venture, and it was he who instilled in me an unshakable conviction that investing is a noble and democratic pursuit. He taught me to believe that successful investing is something everyone can do, and that with a little effort, I could understand any stock as well as anyone else on earth. I only hope that the readers of *Midas Investing* come to share that philosophy.

Contents

Introduction

You can become a great investor.

It doesn't matter if you have no experience in the stock market, or if you haven't done well when you've tried to invest. You don't need extraordinary business acumen, or an advanced degree in accounting or finance. You don't have to be as brilliant as Einstein, or as ambitious as Carnegie.

It's simple, really: As long as you're open-minded and inquisitive, able to learn from your mistakes, and willing to do a little work, you can achieve extraordinary returns in the stock market. Successful investing isn't rocket science. Any reasonably intelligent person can do it.

The goal of this book is to transform you into a great investor— even if you've never before purchased so much as a money-market fund. If you're a beginner, I will teach you the skills that can make you a champion. And if you're already involved in the market, this book can help you refine your technique and can illuminate a sure-fire route to making more money on Wall Street.

Every strategy included in *Midas Investing* is straightforward and practical. I don't intend to make you money by discussing complex dividend-discount models, exotic derivatives, or high-wire options strategies. You can make plenty just by buying and selling basic financial instruments: common stocks and mutual funds. As this book will demonstrate, you don't need to be a daredevil or a genius to find common stocks that will rise by 50%, 100%, 300%, or even 500%.

On any given day, the opportunities are abundant for individuals to make great investments. Many of the best ideas are smaller stocks, companies that are almost anonymous to the average investor.

Fortunately, finding such prospects doesn't take a super investment sleuth. The basic tools to uncover dozens of great stocks are well within your reach. This book will identify those tools and tell you how to use them.

Becoming a great investor can change your life, and not only in the most obvious material ways. You'll be able to improve your standard of living dramatically. But, apart from the dollars and cents, successful investing is a deeply satisfying experience in and of itself. It's like climbing a mountain or running a marathon. Just doing it gives you a profound sense of personal accomplishment.

That's because hunting for great stocks is endlessly stimulating and challenging. It is an intellectual process full of nuance. Reasoning skills are constantly tested, and analytical assumptions must be shaped and reshaped against a perpetually changing backdrop.

In short, investing is truly one of life's great games. It is just plain fun. And it pays a lot better than bridge or backgammon.

Today is an extraordinary time for individual investors. Why? Because we're in the midst of a genuine investing information explosion. Whether the information is circulated in print or comes from television or the new electronic media, it is accessible, plentiful, and affordable.

I'll discuss these information sources, and the ways you can use them, throughout *Midas Investing*. But the upshot of it all is this: Individual investors now have more power and more profit-making potential than ever before.

In an earlier era, only affluent people had enough resources and contacts to stay in the know. In the early nineteenth century, for example, Nathan Rothschild made a killing in the financial markets after his fleet of carrier pigeons delivered him the news of Britain's upset victory at Waterloo.

Rothschild's great advantage was that his expensive birds were faster than the fleetest ship carrying word to London trading floors. As the first man in England to know of Wellington's great victory, Rothschild began buying every stock in sight.

At the time, most British traders were anticipating defeat and oc-cupation—and dumping shares at fire-sale prices. Days later, when the news finally reached Britain that Napoleon had been defeated, the stock market soared, and Rothschild emerged a wealthier man than ever.

Today, you don't need a squadron of birds to keep abreast of the news. Now, everyone—rich or poor—can get low-cost, high-quality information about thousands and thousands of stocks.

Information moves markets, and an individual investor today can be better informed about a particular company than J. P. Morgan was in his heyday.

I'll be teaching you a simple system for finding and profiting from the thousands of great investing opportunities that await you daily. I don't use the word "simple" loosely. Many investors go astray because they've been hooked by advice that makes investing more complicated than it is.

Investing isn't brain surgery. Nor is success in the financial mar-kets dependent on mystical, God-given stock-picking talent. It doesn't matter whom you know, how much money you start with, or how well you did at school.

What does matter is finding a system that works for you. There's no one-and-only path, but, by studying great investors, I've discov-ered that all of them—no matter what their style—employ a clearly articulated system for selecting and rejecting stocks. And these great investors have the discipline to follow their rules no matter how the overall market is performing.

Midas Investing describes the systematic approach that works for me. I'll discuss in detail the key elements that I rely on—rapid earn-ings growth, insider buying, price momentum, investment themes, and portfolio monitoring. I'll demonstrate how I have profited from them. More important, I'll show you how they can work for you.

Before you can achieve maximum returns, you'll have to put aside a lot of the conventional "wisdom" about individual investors and the stock market. There's a good reason to put it aside. It's wrong—so spectacularly wrong that it creates enormous opportunities for individual investors.

A number of prevailing myths about investing infuriate me because they prevent millions of investors from making as much money in stocks as they could. Three particularly irksome fallacies are:

1. The deck is stacked against individual investors.

2. Small-cap stocks (companies with total share values below $500 million) are much more dangerous than so-called blue chips.

3. Individuals can't get access to the investing information that is essential to success.

I spend almost all of my investing time focusing on small-cap and micro-cap stocks. That's where I find more opportunities for maximum returns. It's also easier to make money off a small stock than a big one.

The reason? Because the market in small stocks is much less *efficient* than the market for large, highly visible stocks. (In an efficient market, all information about a company is factored into the price of its stock every day. In an inefficient market, bargains exist because stock prices do not fully reflect all available information about a company. Inefficiency creates opportunity.)

The stocks of many thriving small-cap companies are mispriced largely because so few people know about them. I believe that Wall Street institutions and the popular press, in their bias against these companies, have exaggerated the risks and underestimated the rewards of small-cap investing. They've scared many people away.

But there is more to this popular ignorance than a tale of exaggerated risks. Wall Street's a strange world, and one of the strangest things about it is that almost every institution follows the same universe of stocks. Instead of looking at all 10,000 publicly traded stocks, they generally follow the largest 1,000 and ignore the rest.

There's a certain logic to this approach. Mental flexibility is required to analyze these stocks effectively, and too many institutional research departments are hidebound in their ways. More important, the sheer size of even a middle-of-the-road institutional portfolio makes it almost pointless for a manager to spend time searching for hot small stocks. An institution trying to invest hundreds of millions of dollars could never buy enough of a very tiny stock to make a difference in the institution's overall performance record.

What that means, in effect, is that institutions give their portfolio managers marching orders to avoid many of the best stocks in America.

Imagine a brilliant portfolio manager contemplating Chrysler, MicroTouch, and Colonial Data, three great companies that *Individual Investor* has recommended in recent years. This guru can buy Chrysler, which is large and liquid, with 382 million shares outstanding and a total market value of $20 billion.

No matter how smart the manager, MicroTouch (the nation's leading maker of touch screens for computers and automated teller machines) or Colonial Data (a fast-growing producer of telephone caller-identification systems) probably wouldn't get a nod. For the average money manager, the total market value of MicroTouch ($170 million) or Colonial Data ($140 million) is just too small to bother with. That's too bad for our hypothetical manager, considering that MicroTouch shares have appreciated by more than 350% since November 1992, and Colonial Data is up 467% since November 1993.

Does this mean that the world of small-cap investing is really a level playing field? Actually, it's better than level. The field is tilted in favor of the small investor who does some homework.

What about the high risks so many people associate with small caps? That association is valid in only the narrowest sense. Yes, a single small-cap stock is more vulnerable to calamity than a Microsoft or a Procter & Gamble. But even the biggest and best-known companies can suffer staggering one-day—or prolonged—declines. Over the past few years, investors have lost millions when such household names as General Motors, Philip Morris, and IBM nosedived.

But there is a time-tested way to protect against the greater volatility of small caps: by building a portfolio of at least ten different small-cap stocks. If one of the stocks gets obliterated by unexpected bad news—and I'd be lying if I told you this never happens—the performance of the other stocks in the portfolio should more than compensate for the big loser.

By accepting more volatility in individual stocks, you can improve your overall performance. Keep in mind that small-cap stocks are statistically *better* than their large-cap cousins. On a risk/reward basis, the small-cap universe remains undervalued.

Since 1926, the S&P 500 (Wall Street's benchmark stock index, published by Standard & Poor's; it contains shares representing more than two-thirds of the entire market's total value) has returned 10.6% a year with dividends reinvested. During the same period, small-cap stocks have returned 12.2% a year, according to a landmark study by Ibbotson Associates, the Chicago-based research firm. (I wasn't kidding when I said that many Wall Street professionals are forbidden to buy the best-performing stocks in the market.)

That 1.6% difference is bigger than you may think. After a decade of 10.6% returns, with the dividends reinvested in more shares, a $10,000 portfolio would grow to $27,387. At 12.2% it would grow to $31,618. Stretch the comparison out for 20 years and the respective values would be $74,940 versus $99,888.

And *you* can do even better than a 12.2% compounded annual return. A disciplined and selective investor can make 25% to 30% a year with common stocks. I truly believe that's a realistic goal.

Why? Because I've managed to achieve it during my investing career. And I've seen other small-cap investors reap equally outsized rewards.

What about the "comfort factor" you supposedly get with blue chips? Frankly, it's an illusion. To begin with, blue chips have never been as safe as Wall Street likes to suggest. True, they may not fall as fast as small caps can. But when they do fall, look out below. IBM was $170 in 1987; in 1993, it hit $40. In 1993 and 1994, Bethlehem Steel shed nearly half its value in a twelve-month period. In 1993, Philip Morris plummeted from $85 to $45 in a few months; a stunning 25% decline was recorded in a single day.

What about the argument that when you buy blue chips you can always be sure that any downdraft is temporary? Tell that joke to any longtime holder of Polaroid. In 1973, you could have sold Polaroid for $120. It would have been a good move, because today it's $47.13. The list of "blue-chip" disasters—Woolworth, Western Union, Kodak, Xerox, Continental Illinois, Penn Central—goes on and on.

What about the notion that individuals cannot possibly know as much about a company as the pros do? Sometimes, this is true. It's hard to imagine that any small investor could ever know as much about the different parts of IBM as one of the 54 Wall Street analysts paid to follow the company every day.

In fact, with certain exceptions, it's going to be difficult to know enough about any large company to give you an investing edge. And one of my guiding investing principles is to strive for any kind of edge I can get. But part of being a great investor is picking your spots and seeking out situations where your access to information is better than the access of the rest of the pack. How is that possible for individuals? I'll address this subject in detail throughout the book. Let me explain briefly here.

Any investor, no matter how small, can easily get all existing public information about a company. You can get research reports— if any exist—from the analysts who follow the company or from the firm itself. In addition, an individual can talk to company executives directly about sales, earnings, profit margins, insider transactions, acquisitions, and anything else that comes to mind. It may take persistence in some cases, but the rewards are well worth it.

With small companies, it's much easier to get this kind of personal access. Call up a $50 million company with an investment question, and the odds are good that you can talk to the chief financial officer, the chief executive officer, or the chairman of the board. Not only will you get valuable information, but you'll get a sense of the company's management as well. (On the other hand, consider what would happen if you tried to ask IBM chairman Louis Gerstner about the profit margins on mainframes. His assistant's secretary's assistant probably wouldn't take your call.)

Many years ago, my father gave me the most valuable piece of investment advice I've ever received. He told me that if I really did my homework on a company, I could eventually know as much about it as any investor in the country.

This was not an attempt to flatter me. He was trying to make two points. First, you don't need to be a pro to learn all you need to know. Second, in investing, the harder you work, the greater your rewards.

Now I know he was right on both counts. The biggest secret about investing is that the size of your returns is directly proportional to the amount of time and effort you're willing to put into gathering and analyzing information.

To me, that's a terrifically exciting concept. It means that success is not dependent on how much you start with or whom you know. On the contrary, anyone has the opportunity to achieve maximum returns. *You have as much chance as anyone else.*

Unfortunately, millions of individual investors don't believe that statement. When it comes to investing, many bright and confident people suddenly develop inferiority complexes. And is it any wonder that this defeatist outlook is rampant, when so many publications and Wall Street professionals routinely attack the competence of small investors and question why they're even trying to play the game at all?

I'm serious when I say that you can do every bit as well as I have done. You probably won't have the time to research as many stocks as I do, because looking for great investments is my day job. But you don't have to analyze thousands of stocks to be a great investor. A few good ideas a year is enough.

When you finish this book, I want you to know exactly how I helped my subscribers make huge profits in stocks that most pros didn't know existed or couldn't buy even if they wanted to. The long list of non-household-name stocks includes Telescan, Clearly Canadian, Cato Corporation, Michaels Stores, MicroTouch, Seitel, and Colonial Data.

To be sure, I've had my share of enormous losers. But the winners have always made up for the dogs—and then some. Despite a few major clinkers, *Individual Investor*'s annual Magic 25 portfolio rose by 22.5% a year from 1992 to 1994. By contrast, the S&P 500 rose 6.3% per year in that same period. (I apologize if the "Magic 25" name is misleading. There's no magic involved in the selection of these stocks. All are chosen using the criteria and techniques discussed throughout *Midas Investing*.)

The stocks recommended in our *Special Situations Report* newsletter have been even more magical. From 1991 to 1994, they rose 221%. Only two newsletters in the country did better during that time period, according to the *Hulbert Financial Digest*, an independent newsletter rating service.

I believe that you can maximize your returns by seeking stocks that could double in eighteen months. That's the way to achieve an overall return of 20%, 30%, or 40% a year. I certainly don't look for stocks that will go up 10% or 15% in a good year. Both types of stocks could decline, but I want the risk/reward ratio working in my favor.

You may not believe this, but many of you are already closer to becoming outstanding investors than you realize. In investing, as in many other things, the gap between the also-ran and the all-star isn't nearly as wide as you might expect.

Achievement is incremental. As Kevin Costner points out in the baseball movie *Bull Durham*, one hit a week is all that separates a big leaguer from someone whose career ends in Triple A. That's the difference between a .250 hitter in the minors and a .300 slugger on his way to the major leagues.

To become a superior investor, you need only a few extra singles and doubles, and a couple of home runs. One hit a week and your whole life is different.

Concentrating on small caps is one way to get the extra hits. That's where you have a real edge, because the majority of public companies are woefully underfollowed by the professional investment community. This realization gave me the idea to create *Individual Investor*.

Here are the facts. There are approximately 10,000 public companies in the United States, and 3,000 of them are listed on the Pink Sheets (a collection of relatively illiquid, mostly tiny stocks that are notoriously difficult to trade). About 70% of the remaining 7,000 companies—or approximately 5,000 companies—have a market cap of less than $250 million; 55% have a market cap of less than $100 million. Small stocks, but big numbers. And they represent enormous profit potential for investors. From that list of 5,000 stocks will emerge the next Microsoft, Wal-Mart, or Apple Computer.

Some institutions operate in the small-cap world, but relatively few enter the realm of the microcaps. There are more than 6,000 mutual funds in America, but only about two dozen micro-cap funds (focusing on stocks with market values under $150 million), and most of them have small asset bases. That's an astonishing fact. It means that more than 99.5% of the nation's funds are ignoring the majority of publicly traded companies. To my mind, that's an incredible waste of resources. But it creates more opportunity for me—and for the readers of this book.

If you were put off by my assertion that effort leads to reward, don't be. The amount of work needed to become a well-informed investor may be less than you imagined. It certainly doesn't have to be a full-time job, and it should be enjoyable.

To illustrate how the process can work, let me show you briefly what led *Individual Investor* to recommend Telescan, one of our biggest winners. In the spring of 1993, we noticed that Microsoft co-founder and successful technology investor Paul Allen had purchased $1 million worth of Telescan stock, about 7% of the total shares. That big a purchase by an individual with an exceptional track record always leads us to find out more.

In this case, I was especially curious because I was already a very satisfied user of the company's sophisticated investment analysis software. But I wondered: How big can the market for this kind of software be?

We then began formal research by calling the company to get a complete package of financial information. We liked what we learned about revenue trends and new product development. Telescan was not yet making money from its investment software, but that product was not where management thought major future growth would be. The firm had developed other leading-edge interactive software and had formed marketing alliances with some major partners.

We then talked to management and found responses forthcoming and reasonable. (No matter what executives tell you, though, don't ever let yourself be seduced by rosy projections. At all times, try to think for yourself.)

Furthermore, we liked the fact that the stock was directly connected to a big investment theme, the emergence of the information superhighway. We didn't know whether tiny Telescan would ever become a major player in that market. That, however, wasn't the immediate question we were trying to answer. We wanted to know about the short term.

Our investigation suggested that Telescan was about to experience a power surge in revenue, which we hoped would lead to substantial profits. *Individual Investor* first recommended the stock at $2.50 in 1993. By the end of the year, it had quadrupled to $10.

If you've never done any independent research before, I have a suggestion. Get your feet wet by contacting one or more of the five companies listed below. Ask for their financials (the term "financials" refers to a company's annual report and recent quarterly reports, as well the forms 10-K and 10-Q filed with the federal government). I've chosen these companies because you'll be likely to relate either to what they do or how they present information to shareholders.

1. **Berkshire Hathaway** (402-346-1400). Chairman Warren Buffett's annual report is legendary for its wit and investment insights.

2. **Chrysler** (313-956-5741). This is a company in an industry you probably understand quite well.

3. **Individual Investor Group** (212-843-2777). The company publishes my magazine and newsletters. We make a conscious effort to make our annual report as helpful to investors as possible. If you call, ask for Margaret.

4. **Inter-visual Books** (310-396-8708). This little company's annual report is designed in the style of a children's pop-up book. Besides being extremely entertaining, Inter-visual's annual report gives you a great impression of what the company does, which is publish pop-up books.

5. **Marvel Entertainment Group** (212-696-0808). Like Inter-visual Books, Marvel Entertainment, the nation's leading comic book publisher, communicates vividly what it does and how management thinks. Your kids will love the annual report—if you let them see such things.

You'll probably be surprised at how much you'll learn on your own from this material, even if you don't read every word of each document. In Chapter 2, I'll discuss in detail what you can hope to find out from the various legally required disclosures of public companies. The important point for now is: Discover how easy it is to get important information about any company that interests you.

If you follow the methods I describe, you'll learn about dozens of companies that will appeal to you. Many of them will be excellent investing opportunities. And by following the advice set forth in the chapters of this book, you'll find out about these potential big winners long before other investors do.

MIDAS
INVESTING

1

Investing Isn't Brain Surgery

A FIVE-STEP STRATEGY

I'll acknowledge up front that I had more than a few advantages during my own investing education. I come from an investing family. At an earlier age than most, I was exposed to the principles of investing by my father, the financier Saul Steinberg.

Dad's an extraordinary man. He's been tremendously successful in business and as an investor, and he is an able and enthusiastic teacher. But, of all the insights I've gained from my father over the years, the most important investing lesson he ever taught me was also one of the first: If you gather the right information and use it correctly and aggressively, you can make a lot of money investing. It doesn't matter how old you are, or how much capital you begin with. Persistence and common sense are the most important tools of a successful investor.

That kind of old-fashioned advice may seem quaint. After all, we live in an era when ever more complex investing practices hold sway on Wall Street. From derivatives based six siblings away from the underlying equity to black-box algorithmic trading, the professional investment community has moved boldly to the arcane frontiers of high science. Trying to make money in plain-vanilla common stocks?

The fashionable financial set would sooner be seen wearing knickers and beaver-skin topcoats.

Let them keep their advanced mathematical formulas, I say. You can make a lot more money, much more easily, by investing in traditional stocks and mutual funds.

They come in all shapes and sizes. When I was much younger, I focused primarily on larger companies. My key research tools were business magazines like *Forbes* and *Business Week*, as well as the indispensable *Value Line Investment Survey*. I remember vividly how they helped lead me to my first successful investment.

About the time of my bar mitzvah, I became fascinated by something I read about Abbott Laboratories in *Forbes*. According to analysts, Abbott's product line was full of attractive offerings, yet a statistical comparison of the stock versus its industry peers showed that investors weren't giving Abbott the credit it was due. Other drug companies were trading at much higher valuations, and I knew there might be opportunity to profit from the discrepancy.

The company looked cheap and its growth prospects seemed extraordinary. Quite a combination. I then turned to *Value Line*'s report on the company and became more convinced of Abbott's attractiveness. Even at the age of 13, it looked great to me.

So, with my parents' permission, I took my bar mitzvah money and bought the stock. Nine months later, after a gain of 40%, I sold my holdings. I was hooked on investing and have never looked back.

(Actually, I did look back a little. In the 17 years since I sold Abbott, the stock has risen 1,200%. I did well, but I could have done even better. This was my first lesson about the toughest issue in investing—when to sell. The second lesson: When you find a truly great company in an expanding market, the best strategy is often just to buy and hold.)

Value Line helped me find other great stocks. I didn't, of course, repeat my Abbott Labs experience with each successive investment. Even so, I did pretty well as a young investor. Spending time with *Value Line* became a predictable joy.

Every Friday, the new *Value Line* would arrive in the mail, with updated reports on 200 companies. Before the weekend was over, I would have read every report.

For me, it was a labor of love. Once I learned how to interpret the dry, statistical language of a standard *Value Line* company profile, I understood that each compact page tells a complex, provocative story. As a teenager, I enjoyed them as much as my comic books.

When I went off to college, this habit amused my classmates. Even among Wharton undergraduates, it was considered eccentric in the extreme to take such a fanatical interest in stocks. On Fridays after class, I'd rush home to get the mail. My friends would compare my excitement about the arrival of *Value Line* to Steve Martin's jubilant response, in the movie *The Jerk*, to the annual arrival of the telephone directory. "The new phone book is here!" he'd shout. "The phone book is here!"

As much as I loved the publication, however, the older I got, the more I realized how limited *Value Line* was. Especially for someone who had a growing interest in small-cap stocks.

In 1986, when I was working as an investment banker at Bear Stearns, I became frustrated that information on small companies was so hard to come by. There were more than 5,000 stocks that *Value Line* did not cover. And the publication's scope was broader than most. Almost everybody ignored those companies.

As an investor, however, I was becoming more and more interested in the smallest of the small. These tiny public companies represented the dynamic engines of the American economy, and I knew that there was a lot of money to be made by investing in them and sharing in their growth. Yet, everywhere I turned, traditional sources of financial information acted as if small stocks didn't even exist.

I was determined to get as much information as I could about those stocks. I made a vow that I wouldn't quit until I figured out a way to do it.

Computerized databases were among the most fruitful methods of research. Using a service called Compustat, I did a simple computer search to find all the companies that specialized in providing business data and research. One of the outfits that came up on my screen was Dalton Communications, whose stock was traded on the Pink Sheets.

The name meant nothing to me. Except that I had gone to the Dalton School in Manhattan. Partly based on that fortuitous, and admittedly flimsy, connection, I decided to do a little research into Dalton Communications.

I called the company and learned that it published a monthly newspaper called the *Penny Stock Journal*, whose circulation had peaked at 250,000 in 1985. Since then, however, the publication had been in a steady decline, notwithstanding the spectacular bull market of the 1980s. I became a subscriber.

After about six months, I realized why the publication was losing readers. Almost every stock it featured went down. Many didn't just decline. They swooned, falling by 50% or more in a matter of weeks. A bunch of them went out of business altogether. No guide for short-sellers could have had a better predictive record.

Yet, in spite of such fundamental problems, the *Penny Stock Journal* had established itself as the leading disseminator of information about small-cap and micro-cap stocks, those tiny little companies I was so enamored of.

An obvious question arose: What if a publication analyzed the small-cap market properly, exploring the less efficient corners of the market where tremendous opportunities lay? Wouldn't that be a valuable service for investors?

I bought the *Penny Stock Journal* in 1988, with a goal of bringing independent and professional research to the small-cap area. I thought that if we used the right technology and found hardworking people, we could uncover more outstanding investment ideas than any other publication around. I also saw that our potential audience was much broader than just pennystock investors. A short time later, we changed the magazine's name to *Individual Investor* and set about expanding its editorial focus.

We started with about 25,000 subscribers. Today, *Individual Investor* has nearly 200,000—and the number is rising steadily. A big part of the magazine's appeal is that we have consciously designed it to be straightforward and user-friendly. We have also built as "smart" a publication as we could. To do that, I carefully analyzed my own investment techniques and decided to recreate my investment approach in the magazine.

Exactly what was I looking for when I tried to discover tomorrow's hot stocks? With 7,000 stocks out there, what tools was I using to narrow the field so I'd focus on the best opportunities and leave the dogs alone?

By distilling my own methods, I ended up with the five-part stock selection system that guides the magazine and forms the backbone of this book:

1. Earnings.

2. Insider buying.

3. Momentum investing.

4. Updates.

5. Themes and sectors.

Each of the five approaches is discussed in much greater detail in its own chapter, but I'd like to introduce you briefly to the methodology. An overview is important here to make it clear that the five different approaches can often work together. Or, put another way, the different techniques can give you a second, third, fourth, or fifth chance to find a stock with great potential.

EARNINGS

More than 7,000 public companies report earnings every quarter, which means there are about 30,000 earnings announcements every year. How can you possibly stay on top of all of them?

You can't; but you can make it a habit to scan the list of the companies reporting the best earnings gains each day or each month. In every issue, the newspaper *Investor's Business Daily* publishes a table ranking the companies that reported earnings the previous day. For this list, the sheer size of a company's earnings is immaterial. All that matters is the percentage gain in earnings compared to last year (listed by quarter).

Each month, in the "America's Fastest Growing Companies" section of *Individual Investor*, we take the same information and present it somewhat differently. Determined to devote space only to those companies whose profit growth is among the very best in the country, we produce complete earnings information on every company reporting an earnings gain of 100% or more.

Are we setting too high a growth hurdle for companies? Yes and no. The formula does eliminate some great stocks from consideration. (The companies showing earnings growth of 70%, 80%, and 90% aren't necessarily being completely ignored. We often spotlight them in different sections of the magazine.) Over time, however, creating such a high standard offers us more downside protection and produces significantly higher returns. The stocks highlighted in this section have turned in spectacular results.

Great earnings reports routinely lead me to companies I had never heard of before. One example is CDW Computer Centers, a Northbrook, Illinois, marketer of computers and computer-related equipment. In September 1993, we featured the company largely because of its great numbers. In the quarter ended June 30, 1993, earnings per share jumped from $0.17 to $0.84. Almost as impressive, though, was the fact that sales soared by 45%, to $61.8 million.

We weren't just mesmerized by the numbers. After talking to the company and analyzing its business, we discovered that it operates in an alluring niche and has an effective growth strategy in place. Essentially, CDW is a direct marketer specializing in the home and small business markets, two of the fastest-growing sectors of the computer hardware business in the mid-1990s. The company's stated business philosophy is to be a low-cost marketer supplying superior sales advice and customer service. That's one of the most powerful one-two punches you can have in the business arena.

We recommended CDW shares at $15.50. Then, as often happens with a company that has reported a blowout quarter, earnings continued to grow at an extraordinary rate that exceeded analysts' expectations. (Paul Wick, of the Seligman mutual fund family, refers to this as the "cockroach theory" of earnings surprises: Where you see one cockroach, there are probably many more. The same rule seems to apply to earnings surprises. They tend not to be isolated events.) The next quarter, CDW's earnings jumped 82% over the previous year. The quarter after, they rose by 81% more.

Predictably, the stock rocketed up as well. In early 1995, just sixteen months after we wrote about it, CDW hit $39, a gain of 152% from the price where we spotted it.

INSIDER BUYING

Few investors have better track records than corporate insiders. When an officer, director, or major shareholder increases his or her stake in a company, good corporate news often lies ahead.

Smart investors have to pay attention to what corporate insiders are doing. In fact, some of my best investment ideas have come from this source, which explains why we include four pages of detailed information on insider transactions in every issue of *Individual Investor*.

One of the great things about insider buying is that you can often learn about fabulous situations well before any good news has been announced. That means you can acquire shares at a lower price, in advance of any stock price run-up. (By the time a company has announced terrific earnings or the development of an important new product, the market will have already bid up the price of that company's stock. The stock may still go much higher, but the odds are slim that you'll be getting in near the low.)

An example: When chairman Fred Prins and other insiders began buying shares of Prins Recycling in February 1994, a casual observer might have assumed they were nuts. The Boston-based company, whose lone asset was a single materials-recovery facility (a fancy name for a recycling plant), was a bad bet if you used classic balance sheet or cash flow analysis.

The company had $8 million in annual revenues and was losing money. Its balance sheet was dreadful. The stock, which had been as high as $3.88 in 1993, was trading for $1.25 when Prins, who already owned 56%, began increasing his stake. Other insiders soon followed his lead. Instead of wondering whether they had taken leave of their senses, we asked our standard insider buying question: "What do they know that we don't?"

The answer to that question was fascinating—and enormously valuable. The insiders believed that earnings were about to turn around, they thought that new recycling contracts were on the way. They also suspected (correctly) that the prices paid for recycled paper would continue to rise, and they knew that the company was about to embark on an ambitious acquisition strategy.

The stock might have gained based on any one of these assumptions. When all four turned out to be accurate, it was a recipe for a perfect investment soufflé. Prins reported positive earnings the next quarter, and the stock jumped to $3.00 by August 1994. By October it was trading between $5.00 and $6.00 per share.

In November 1994, we made it a 1995 Magic 25 selection at a price of $5.38, and the good news kept flowing. By February 1995, the stock had risen past $9. After reporting another quarter of great earnings in April, the stock hit $18.75.

The fourteen-month gain? An incredible 1,400% from the point at which the insider buying began. (Many months later, severe disruptions in its core business caused Prins to crumble back. Nonetheless, the short-term success of Prins is illustrative of a powerful investment thesis.)

Besides playing golf with the chairman, the only possible way to notice Prins near its lows was to pay attention to insider buying. The stock had absolutely no visibility. No analyst followed it. No newsletter recommended it. The only people who seemed to think it was a worthwhile investment were the folks who ran the company. Everyone else completely ignored it.

MOMENTUM INVESTING

This may be the most controversial of my five investing strategies. Momentum investing, as you may know, already has a bad name in some circles. To some of its more extreme adherents, the strategy amounts to little more than this: If a stock is going up, buy it. If it starts going down, dump it.

Looked at that way, we're talking about nothing more subtle than a technically sophisticated variation on the greater fool theory. Under this "strategy," investors buy a stock simply because they believe they can soon sell it to someone more gullible.

That is *not* what I mean by momentum investing.

Here's how I define the technique. Start with the obvious. The best-performing stocks are featured on the new highs list published every week in *Barron's*. It is impossible for the big winners to fail to show up on the *Barron's* list.

In addition, market history makes it clear that stocks in a sharp uptrend often continue to advance quickly. The glorious interval may be relatively brief but, at least for a while, these stocks do wonderfully.

This does not mean that an investor should indiscriminately buy every stock—or just *any* stock. The stocks on the list may be good ones (great earnings, a hot new product, or savvy new management) or they may be bad ones (outrageous hype, a short squeeze, or inevitable stock group rotation). But whatever the case, it's very profitable to sift through the new highs to find out what is propelling a particular stock skyward. One of the highs may well be an otherwise anonymous small-cap stock poking its head up to be seen.

For example, in the March 1995 "Hot Stocks" section of *Individual Investor*, we wrote about a company called PC DOCS. The only reason it came to our attention was because it started showing up on the new highs list. Repeatedly.

The stock had already risen from a low of $0.44 to $1.94 by the time we wrote about it, but we decided to recommend it nonetheless because the company's prospects looked so alluring.

PC DOCS (for *d*ocument *o*rganization and *c*ontrol *s*ystem) sells software packages that manage activity on a computer network. Any company that makes networks easier to use has the potential to earn a ton of money. In this case, it was clear that people unrelated to PC DOCS had warmly endorsed its software. It had won *PC Magazine's* Editor's Choice award for best document management software three years out of four:

The Toronto-based company was a leader in a hot market and had just landed a large contract that would bring it sizable profits and better industry recognition. The stock was rising for the right reasons. An impressive list of customers had climbed aboard, including the U.S. General Accounting Office, Canada's Treasury Board Secretariat and Department of Finance, and Du Pont (which has 114,000 employees).

According to the Gartner Group (a major technology market researcher), PC DOCS holds a 15% to 20% share of a market expected to grow ninefold by 1997. Thus, even if its market share remained stable, revenues could increase dramatically in the next three years. And if it gained market share? The math could then get very interesting.

The performance of PC DOCS' stock did quickly become quite interesting, indeed. The company announced terrific earnings and its fourth *PC Magazine* award. In less than three months, the stock ran from $1.94 to $9.00, a phenomenal gain of 364%.

UPDATES

Nothing endures but change, the saying goes. In the life of a corporation, things change frequently—and quickly. The best investors try to stay on top of these transformations.

One of the greatest pieces of investment counsel ever given is, unfortunately, one of the hardest to follow emotionally. The advice?

With all your holdings, repeatedly ask: Given what I know today, would I still buy a particular stock?

The question addresses a basic investing truth in a profound way. Your analysis may have been right six months ago, but are you still correct today? Have the unpredictable events of the past six months made you feel better about your purchase, or worse?

Many investors find it quite difficult to answer these questions, for a number of reasons:

1. It takes some work, including retracing a fair number of the original decision steps.

2. The reevaluation process (Should I buy? Sell? Hold?) can be complex.

3. Revisiting a buy decision might make investors realize that they didn't know as much as they should have when they bought the shares in the first place.

But asking these questions is a wonderful, and ultimately very profitable, habit. If you own a stock, you're presumably paying attention to its announcements about earnings, new products, and management shifts. Just apply critical intelligence to the new information you receive. How does it compare to your expectations? Do the company's comments indicate that management is more positive—or considerably more negative—about future prospects than it was six or twelve months ago?

This update process is especially valuable when applied to the stocks on an investor's "watch list." The watch list is a crucial investment tool. For me, it contains stocks I find intriguing but have not yet purchased because the shares are too speculative, too expensive, or, for one reason or another, too problematic.

I need to feel more comfortable before I buy in. I need to know, for instance, whether a company's brilliant new product or strategy actually shows signs of working in the marketplace. Always, I'm eager to know what kind of expectations management is trading on: How big? How fast? How dominant? And most important of all, when?

At any time, it's smart to have three, or six, or ten stocks on your watch list. Pay attention to the news that flows from these companies. Is the story playing out as you hoped or is the company running into unexpected problems? Be patient and take action only when an update causes you to upgrade a "watch" into a "buy."

We've had great success with McAfee Associates—twice. The second time was a classic update play.

At the time of our initial recommendation, McAfee, based in Santa Clara, California, was one of the world's leading suppliers of antivirus software, which keeps computer programs operating at peak efficiency. That's a fantastically profitable niche, but, by late 1993, Wall Street had decided that McAfee was so dominant within its core business segment, it had few prospects for further earnings growth.

In our January 1994 issue, we chose McAfee as one of our Magic 25 stocks because, at a depressed price of $6.25, it had become a value stock. In other words, it was priced like some aging, low-growth industrial company, not a dynamic, high-growth technology concern. At the time we featured it, McAfee was trading at just ten times earnings, despite some of the widest profit margins we had ever seen and a balance sheet that was accordingly loaded with cash.

A year later, the stock was $14, a gain of 124%. Was its success simply a matter of other investors catching up with our superior reasoning? Not exactly.

A close look told us that more than the stock price had changed. McAfee had a new CEO who, over the previous year, had transformed what was formerly a one-product company. Antiviral software would still be crucial to McAfee's future, but, through acquisitions and internal product development, the new boss had turned the company into a powerhouse in the network management software arena.

As this new corporate strategy began to translate into growing sales and profits, we reevaluated McAfee. Yes, the stock had already doubled, but this past performance wasn't relevant to the question at hand. Based on its new strategy and growth prospects, was McAfee— now at $14—still undervalued?

We answered with an emphatic yes: McAfee was selling at fifteen times our 1995 earnings estimates, a valuation 50% lower than that of comparable software companies. The market still hadn't acknowledged how different McAfee was. So we told readers to buy more shares.

Within four months, the shares had hit $31, an increase of 121%. Total gain in sixteen months: 396%.

I can't emphasize enough how different McAfee was the second year. *It wasn't the same company.* If we hadn't figured out how different McAfee really was, we might have settled for a quick 100% profit and moved on. It would have been a costly mistake.

THEMES AND SECTORS

On Wall Street, they say, "The trend is your friend," a reference to the fact that, more often than not, a rising market continues to rise and a declining market finds new ways to sag.

A trend can be your ally in a different way as well. If you understand a broad economic cycle or an enormously important industry development, you can have an edge over other investors.

Let's look at the "information superhighway." This is a definite trend. But you won't be successful investing in the digital future if you simply throw money at it. Instead, the way to profit is to realize exactly how the trend benefits individual companies, and then reach your own conclusion about which companies' strategies make the most sense.

In 1995, I made a lot of money buying the stocks of companies that provide access to the Internet. I didn't completely understand the technology, but I knew how important that access was. And I could tell how excited the public and the press were about the potential of online communications as a medium.

When you try to play a trend like this, you start with an advantage that can quickly turn into a liability. The issue is hype. Every hot new area will eventually become overhyped. That's how things work in America. And when the enthusiasm is at fever pitch, it is a given that many companies in the sector—perhaps all companies in the sector—will be overvalued.

In this climate, two strategies make sense:

1. Get in and get out, before the crowd.

2. If you're determined to make a long-term commitment to the sector, don't be shaken out by the first stunning decline.

(Note: I'll address this idea in much greater detail later, but one of the best and safest ways to play a trend is to buy the nuts-and-bolts industry suppliers whose success isn't dependent on a particular brand name. For example, in wireless communications, three of the biggest winners of the 1990s have been: (1) Three-Five Systems, provider of liquid crystal displays for cellular phones and other electronics products; (2) Wireless Telecom, tester of cellular phones' ability to suppress background noise; and (3) Glenayre Technologies, which makes display chips for pagers.)

Realize as well that a superficial knowledge of trends can be very dangerous. Everyone knows, for instance, that biotechnology seems to represent the pharmaceutical wave of the future. Terrific. The problem is, this knowledge alone doesn't help an investor separate the winners from the disasters in biotech. Most development-stage biotech drugs are almost impossible for a layperson to assess. And the general trend won't bail you out if the company you chose to invest in is denied FDA approval for its new drug.

Generally, it's smarter to focus on an individual stock and see how it fits into a major trend, rather than seize on a trend and scramble to find a company that will allegedly profit from it.

Our best Magic 25 selection of 1994 was New Milford, Connecticut-based Colonial Data Technologies, the nation's leading supplier of Caller ID services. When we recommended the shares at $2.25, sales and earnings were growing sharply and we liked management's expansion philosophy. The stock was trading at nineteen times estimated 1994 earnings—a very low multiple, given the industry's spectacular growth and prospects.

Growth was exploding even though the Caller ID service had not yet been approved in many states, including California. Approval was likely, however, and we felt it would give the shares a boost when it came. Another attraction was that, although competition in the sector already existed and was sure to intensify, Colonial Data was the clear technology leader. Its "Block the Blocker" software prevented callers from using a system that would block the Caller ID function.

We also were convinced that the company would benefit from two distinct trends: (1) the growing appeal of new telephone services and (2) the unfortunate rise in concern for personal safety. We thought the wind would be at our back.

We just had no idea how strong the wind would be.

Quarter after quarter, Colonial Data's sales and earnings exceeded our forecasts. We kept raising our estimates, and the stock kept flying. By March 1995, it hit $18.75, giving our subscribers a gain of 733% in fourteen months.

As it turned out, we wouldn't have done too badly if instead we had purchased CIDCO, Colonial Data's primary competitor. In the same fourteen-month period, it rose 105%. Why did we prefer Colonial Data? It was cheaper on a valuation basis, and its "Block the Blocker" feature made its product superior.

The overall trend would have been a friend in either case.

In an ideal world, all five of my indicators would be flashing a buy signal at once. Home Run Enterprises would report that its earnings tripled and insiders increased their holdings as the stock was hitting a new high. At the same time, of course, the company would announce a breakthrough new product—patented, naturally—that would make Internet access easier and cheaper while also halting the aging process.

This could happen, but you might spend a long time waiting. And you might not be so happy when you found what you were seeking. Sometimes the stocks that look too good to be true really are. Very few small companies commit securities fraud, but when they do, you can be sure of one thing. The reported numbers and corporate "news" will be extraordinarily good.

Before you begin this process, realize that you'll find some great companies through each of these five research techniques, but you won't find the same ones on every list at the same time. The world just isn't so simple that every stock can boast every identifying buy signal all at once.

What will happen, though, is that you'll learn how the different approaches work together to improve your investment returns. You'll notice that a company that had heavy insider buying last year just announced its first quarter of great earnings in recent memory. Or perhaps it won FDA approval for a new product that had been in development for years.

Or maybe you'll see that a firm whose progress you've been updating for months has finally begun setting daily new highs. The good news about a company doesn't always come out in a perfectly predictable manner, but the truly great stocks usually have several things in common. At some point, earnings explode. Insiders, if they're smart, increase their holdings. The stock makes the new highs list. The company expands its business—via new products, an acquisition, international growth, and so on—and the outside world of analysts, advisers, and the media begins taking favorable notice of the company. Finally, if the company is truly thriving, its business is often good because it is capitalizing on a major new business opportunity or trend.

Not all roads lead to stock-picking success. But I'm convinced that these five do. The chapters that follow will tell you more about how to use them.

2

The Facts of Life

FINANCIAL BASICS MADE EASY

Americans suffer from a phobia of anything mathematical. The fear is well known and widespread. When we're dealing with financial matters, we become even more frightened. "Investing is too complex," we say. "I'll never get through all those numbers!"

Hogwash. You'll need just three basic financial statements from a company you're interested in: (1) an income statement (also called a profit-and-loss, or P&L), (2) a balance sheet, and (3) a cash flow statement. Any investor—even an inexperienced one—can understand any company's financial statements, no matter how big or complex the firm may be.

To prove this point, we'll analyze in this chapter one of the largest companies in the world, IBM. After doing so, you should be able to take the lessons learned and apply them to any other company's financial statements.

IBM's annual revenues are $64 billion, about 7,000 times the sales of some thriving companies discussed in this book. If you can understand the financials of this vast global company, you can easily repeat the process with stocks that interest you.

Although the numbers in IBM's statements are big, the math isn't difficult. The concepts really aren't that complicated.

The key is to realize that the numbers and the awkward terms you'll encounter are merely the tools that a publicly traded company uses to describe its prospects.

I can absolutely promise you two things from this chapter: (1) You'll learn a lot (for new investors, this may be the most important chapter in the book), and (2) you'll feel great afterward, because you'll be able to understand concepts that seemed intimidating or impenetrable just a short time ago. Sophisticated investors will learn things, too, and may find the section on financial shenanigans particularly illuminating.

Mandatory Public Filings

One reason many companies choose to remain private is that the federal government requires an enormous amount of public disclosure every year. Creating these disclosing documents takes time, energy, and money.

These reports, however, give investors vital information for making decisions. Ideally, an investor should read every public filing by a company in the past twelve months. Only after such due diligence should you actually buy the stock.

The Securities and Exchange Commission (SEC) requires that all public companies—whether IBM or Individual Investor Group—make the following filings every year:

- A 10-K report. This is a complete summary of the company's business and financial condition. No frills, no glossy photos, no chairman's letter. It's more like a prospectus than anything else. Like a prospectus, it addresses risk factors. The report must include an income statement, a balance sheet, and a statement of cash flow.

- Three quarterly reports. Fairly brief documents focusing on business and financial performance in the recently completed quarter.

- A proxy statement. A notice that shareholders receive before they vote on corporate matters such as the election of directors. The statement includes the salaries of inside directors and details about their bonus and stock option plans.

- An annual report. This is often a company's showcase publication, though it is not always the most useful for investors. It generally includes a chairman's letter to shareholders, descriptions of the business and the relevant events of the past year, and a slicker version of the financial documentation that appears in the 10-K report.

- Three quarterly 10-Q reports. Although less comprehensive than the 10-K, these reports contain more information than the quarterly documents routinely sent through the mail. A 10-Q is usually available about 30 days after the standard quarterly report. Like the 10-K, a 10-Q almost never simply materializes in your mailbox. You have to request it. Additional information of value: Disclosures (akin to annual report footnotes) and extremely important data on cash flow.

Whether you're a shareholder or not, the easiest way to get above the documents is through the company's investor relations office. Otherwise, you can get most or all of these reports online or at some public libraries.

THE SCOOP ON IBM

For IBM, the only document we'll examine is the annual report. Let's begin by putting it in context.

The stock was trading at $83 when IBM issued its 1994 annual report in the spring of 1995. Eight years earlier, IBM shares were more than double that price, having hit an all-time high of $175 in 1987. But in 1992 and 1993, the bluest of blue chips announced huge layoffs and shocking losses. By the summer of 1993, the stock had fallen as low as $40. Whatever IBM was—and there was frenzied debate about this—it wasn't what it used to be.

By the time the 1994 annual report appeared, the stock had doubled from its low. Good news had started to flow. Naturally, alert investors wondered: Were years of positive announcements just beginning or was IBM's recovery merely fleeting?

Now on to the report. *Step one:* Ignore all the pretty pictures of products, buildings, and employees.

Step two: Read every word of the chairman's letter to shareholders. Many letters in annual reports are worthless drivel, nothing more than public-relations-driven puff pieces. Still, the chairman's note can help explain a company's position in its industry and its plans for future growth.

If the letter sounds like puffery and recent earnings have been mediocre, avoid the stock. Read enough of these self-aggrandizements and it becomes pretty easy to tell when a chairman is simply trying either to sound optimistic without backup facts or to ignore reality entirely. Pay particular attention to the way the chairman treats bad news. If last year was dreadful, yet the chairman suggests that every single piece of bad news has a silver lining, stop reading and head elsewhere.

As you read, get a sense of how the company met last year's promises. (If they're not itemized, with the results for each promise, read last year's letter as well.) What does the chairman say about the expectations that were *not* met? Does the letter explain what happened or does it simply attribute everything to sinister outside forces or "the economy"?

You don't have to be a chartered financial analyst to judge whether the tone seems candid and credible, or whether the chairman is spouting the corporate equivalent of "My dog ate my homework." (Retailing companies, for example, are notorious for blaming the weather for poor sales. When same-store sales decline, it seems like it's always too warm or too cold to get shoppers into the store.)

The chairman's letter may be most important when a company is in transition, as IBM certainly was in 1995. IBM chairman Lou Gerstner's letter is filled with the kind of even-handed confidence I find appealing. Despite announcing an $11 billion turnaround in 1994 (IBM earned $3 billion after losing $8 billion the previous year, with much of the improvement coming from cost-cutting),

Gerstner says, "We're not an industry leader yet—at least by my definition."

He also points out remaining problems for the company; among them: revenue growth, ability to get products to market quickly, and the need for reengineering. An encouraging sign on the growth front: products introduced in the preceding twelve to eighteen months accounted for almost half of IBM's total hardware revenues.

What's more, Gerstner's expressions of confidence are supported by his actions as an investor. In the middle of 1994, he enlarged his IBM stake by buying more shares on the open market. (By law, insiders like Gerstner must disclose when they buy or sell stock. In Chapter 5, we'll discuss ways to use these filings as investment clues.)

THE INCOME STATEMENT

The income statement reveals the profitability of a company for a specific period and usually contrasts this performance with results in the preceding two years. This spread helps you recognize and analyze trends affecting the bottom line. How fast are sales rising? Are costs under control? Are profit margins increasing or decreasing?

There's no need to get bogged down in the numbers yet. Numbers are simply meant to guide you to what really matters. What trends do you see? Where do potential problems lurk? What great profit opportunities (new products, new markets, new efficiencies) do the numbers suggest?

We'll be going through the numbers—and the relevant definitions—line by line. The income statement details operating results for a specific twelve-month period (in this case, the 1994 calendar year). IBM calls it a *consolidated statement of operations*. At other companies, it may be known as an *earnings report* or *operating statement*.

The capital letters on some lines announce the presence of notes, which function like footnotes but appear later in the text rather than at the bottom of the page. Horrible and wonderful things may be

CONSOLIDATED STATEMENT OF OPERATIONS

International Business Machines Corporation and Subsidiary Companies

(Dollars in millions except per share amounts)

	For the year ended December 31:	Notes	1994	1993	1992
1	*Revenue:*				
2	Hardware sales		$32,344	$30,591	$33,755
3	Software		11,346	10,953	11,103
4	Services		9,715	9,711	7,352
5	Maintenance		7,222	7,295	7,635
6	Rentals and financing	N	3,425	4,166	4,678
7	Total revenue		64,052	62,716	64,523
8	*Cost:*				
9	Hardware sales		21,300	20,696	19,698
10	Software		4,680	4,310	3,924
11	Services		7,769	8,279	6,051
12	Maintenance		3,635	3,545	3,430
13	Rentals and financing		1,384	1,738	1,966
14	Total cost		38,768	38,568	35,069
15	Gross profit		25,284	24,148	29,454
16	*Operating expenses:*				
17	Selling, general and administrative		15,916	18,282	19,526
18	Research, development and engineering	I	4,363	5,558	6,522
19	Restructuring charges	J	–	8,945	11,645
20	Total operating expenses		20,279	32,785	37,693
21	Operating income (loss)		5,005	(8,637)	(8,239)
22	Other income, principally interest		1,377	1,113	573
23	Interest expense	K	1,227	1,273	1,360
24	Earnings (loss) before income taxes		5,155	(8,797)	(9,026)
25	Provision (benefit) for income taxes	H	2,134	(810)	(2,161)
26	Net earnings (loss) before changes in accounting principles		3,021	(7,987)	(6,865)
27	Effect of changes in accounting principles	B	–	(114)	1,900
28	Net earnings (loss)		3,021	(8,101)	(4,965)
29	Preferred stock dividends		84	47	–
30	Net earnings (loss) applicable to common shareholders		$ 2,937	$(8,148)	$(4,965)
	Per share of common stock amounts:				
31	Before changes in accounting principles		$ 5.02	$(14.02)	$(12.03)
32	Effect of changes in accounting principles	B	–	(.20)	3.33
33	Net earnings (loss) applicable to common shareholders		$ 5.02	$(14.22)	$ (8.70)
34	Average number of common shares outstanding: 1994–584,958,699; 1993–573,239,240; 1992–570,896,489				

The notes on pages 52 through 78 are an integral part of this statement.

buried in the notes. That's why the best investors always read them. So should you. You don't have to understand every word to gain insights into a company.

New rules went into effect in 1995. The SEC now allows companies to exclude notes from annual reports (they still have to be submitted to the commission). This can hurt individual investors, but there's a way around the problem. Call the company and ask that anything not included in the new streamlined annual report be sent to you.

Now take a look at what each line reveals about IBM. Lines 2 through 30 represent millions of dollars; the last six digits of the actual amounts have been rounded off and then dropped, to simplify the statement.

❶ *Revenue:*

Line 1. Revenue. The total sales made in the recently concluded fiscal/calendar year. (Some companies' fiscal year ends earlier in the calendar year, not at year-end.) There is no number on this line because some companies, such as IBM, break total revenue into component parts. That information lets you calculate the percentage of total sales accounted for by a segment, and find out how fast it is growing.

❷ Hardware sales $32,344 $30,591 $33,755

Line 2. Hardware sales. Sales grew 6% from 1993 to 1994. A decent forward motion, but far slower than overall computer industry sales, which rose 25% to 30% worldwide during the same period.

❸ Software   11,346   10,953   11,103

Line 3. Software sales. Flat since 1992.

4 Services		9,715	9,711	7,352

Line 4. Services.   Flat versus 1993.

5 Maintenance		7,222	7,295	7,635

Line 5. Maintenance.   Flat versus 1993.

6 Rentals and financing	N	3,425	4,166	4,678

Line 6. Rentals and financing.   Down a significant 18% from 1993. If this were a smaller company, you would have to learn why this happened and what it means. It still matters with IBM, although not nearly as much.

7 Total revenue	64,052	62,716	64,523

Line 7. Total revenue.   The number itself means less than the trend it illustrates. Always figure out how fast revenues have grown over the most recent three-year period.

Let's say revenues grew 15% last year. In an ideal world, you would see increasing gains in these other categories: gross profit, operating profit, net income, and earnings per share.

An excellent report might look something like this:

Revenue	+15%
Gross profit	+20
Operating profit	+24
Net income	+26
Earnings per share	+27

It's also vital to calculate trends in gross margins (line 15 divided by line 7), operating margins (line 21 divided by line 7), and net income margins (line 26 divided by line 7). If all are expanding, that's a great sign. If they're holding steady, that may or may not be acceptable. But beware of companies with declining profit margins. Be sure you understand why the decline is occurring. It often happens in young industries when a company starts facing increased competition. That's not automatically disastrous, but it might suggest that you're too late to enjoy this particular party.

A serious decline can mean that a company has lost its pricing power (perhaps because it no longer has clear product advantages) or that its business is shifting from high-margin products to less profitable commodity-type items.

IBM's overall revenue comparisons are uninspiring, to say the least. Total revenues were down 2.8% in 1993 and up 2.1% in 1994, but not back to the 1992 level. As Gerstner points out in his letter, revenues rose by 6% if the 1993 sales of IBM's Federal Systems Co., which the corporation sold in 1994, are eliminated. Even so, 6% growth is nothing to crow about. To persuade yourself to buy IBM stock, you either have to believe that solid growth will resume or that the company's cost-cutting successes will continue.

What does the chairman say? He believes that IBM can once again become a steady grower. Among his reasons: the company's market—information technology—is a great growth business and the results of its research and development (R&D) efforts (patents and new products) are extremely positive. In 1994, sales at IBM's worldwide open centers (which help customers design and implement client server applications) grew 50% to more than $1 billion. In addition, opportunities in China, Eastern Europe, Asia, and South Africa seem extraordinary. (About 60% of IBM's revenue already comes from abroad.)

As another source of potential growth, Gerstner cites the IBM Global Network, which is the world's largest data network with a presence in 700 cities in more than 100 countries. The company plans to leverage the network as it attempts to command a large portion of the network-centric computing market.

Sounds great, but you can't just take the company's word for it. Read up on IBM. Ask an industry analyst or industry insider how effective a player IBM is in networking and what its future is likely to be. To what extent can you leverage size in this market?

❽ Cost:

Line 8. Cost. Often called cost of sales, this includes labor, overhead, and the cost of materials needed to create finished products. (As you go through each of a company's revenue segments, compare growth in costs to growth in sales.)

❾ Hardware sales	21,300	20,696	19,698

Line 9. Hardware sales. Hardware sales jumped $1.75 billion while costs rose only $604 million—a very good showing.

❿ Software	4,680	4,310	3,924

Line 10. Software. Costs rose about as fast as sales.

⓫ Services	7,769	8,279	6,051

Line 11. Services. Costs declined $510 million while revenues held steady—another good sign.

⓬ Maintenance	3,635	3,545	3,430

Line 12. Maintenance. Costs rose $90 million while sales slipped $73 million. A drop in the bucket for IBM, but I wish it had been the other way around.

⓭ Rentals and financing	1,384	1,738	1,966

Line 13. Rentals and financing. Costs fell $384 million. Looks nice—until you compare it to sales, which slumped $741 million.

⑭ Total cost	38,768	38,568	35,069

Line 14. Total cost. Overall costs rose just $200 million, far less than the revenue gain of $1.34 billion, a powerful indication that IBM has started to do something right.

⑮ Gross profit	25,284	24,148	29,454

Line 15. Gross profit. What you get when you subtract total cost (line 14) from total revenue (line 7). Dividing gross profit by total revenue, we learn that IBM has a 39.5% gross profit margin.

On page 36 of the annual report, IBM states the gross profit margins for 1994, 1993, and 1992. In 1993, gross margin was 38.5%; in 1992, it was 45.6%.

⑯ *Operating expenses:*			

Line 16. Operating expenses. All additional costs of running the company that are *not* covered on line 14 show up here.

⑰ Selling, general and administrative	15,916	18,282	19,526

Line 17. Selling, general, and administrative. Commonly known as "SG&A," this expense line typically covers salaries and commissions of salespeople, advertising and promotion, travel and entertainment, office payroll, and executive salaries. Many companies that have cut costs have started here. On the downside, this is the "overhead" line that often starts expanding just as a company begins losing control over its expenses.

At IBM, the dramatic decline from 1992 to 1994 is hard to miss. SG&A expenses dropped $3.6 billion in two years, with most of the decline coming in 1994. That represents an 18% reduction. Much of the cost-cutting reflects the enormous layoffs that began in 1992.

⑱ Research, development and engineering	I	4,363	5,558	6,522

Line 18. Research, development, and engineering. Just what it sounds like—all the costs of developing and testing products before they come to market. Again, there has been a huge drop—an astonishing 33%—since 1992. That's real cutting, but it is not automatically good news.

Normally, I like to see technology companies devote 10% to 16% of their revenues to R&D. In 1992, IBM's R&D spending was 10% of revenues, right at the low end of the range. Currently, it's 7%. This kind of cut can make earnings look good today while seriously jeopardizing a company's future. This fact alone might scare some investors away.

The chairman's letter helps ease my concern. The issue is never simply how much you spend. The quantifiable results you generate are what matters. Superficially, IBM seems to be surviving the R&D budget cuts quite well. Gerstner notes that, in 1994, IBM was number one in winning U.S. patents for the second year in a row. Its 1,298 patents in 1994 were the most ever issued to any company in a single year. Furthermore, much of the cost-cutting eliminated redundancies. If this were a small technology company, I'd be much more nervous if I saw R&D spending fall from 10% to 7%. To me, that smells like a desperate attempt to pump up earnings or conserve cash—to look good this year while mortgaging the future.

Note 1 breaks down research, development, and engineering spending into component parts.

⑲ Restructuring charges	J	–	8,945	11,645

Line 19. Restructuring charges. This lofty term reflects one-time charges for laying off workers (and handing out severance packages), closing plants, writing off inventory, and similar actions.

It's always important to know what earnings would have been without the restructuring charges. This simple calculation is called "backing out" the charges. (You can do it with any one-time event.) There are no restructuring charges for 1994, but if you were analyzing the 1993 report and wanted to know IBM's earnings without the special charges, you'd subtract line 19 from line 20 to arrive at operating expenses of $23,840. Add to that the total cost on line 14, then subtract the total from line 7. The answer is $308 million, or $0.54 per share (573 million shares were outstanding in 1993; see line 34), a number clearly open to interpretation.

Stated as a price (of the stock)-to-earnings (P/E) ratio, the result is dreadful. Say the stock price is $55 per share, with 573 million shares issued. Multiply $55 by 573 million shares, then divide by $308 million. The P/E ratio is 102. Given the doomsday headlines about IBM at that time, 102 was not too bad. It meant that, during some of its darkest days, IBM avoided breaking even and could still make some money.

Note J explains the restructuring charges spread over 1992 and 1993. Of the $20.5 billion in total charges for the two years, $11.5 billion covered workforce-related expenses (layoffs, early retirement deals, and so on), $4.9 billion involved reductions in manufacturing capacity, $3.4 billion was spent on shedding excess space, and $700 million was unspecified.

Note J also says that IBM has $2.3 billion of restructuring charges it hasn't allocated yet. (For tax or accounting reasons, firms sometimes spread out these charges over a few years.) Approximately $1.3 billion in restructuring reserves were to be used by March 31, 1995, and the remainder by December 31, 1995. The 1995 annual report, therefore, should show $2.3 billion in restructuring charges.

⑳ Total operating expenses	20,279	32,785	37,693

Line 20. Total operating expenses. The sum of lines 17, 18, and 19. For 1994, this shows the impact of cost-cutting and the absence of a restructuring charge.

㉑ Operating income (loss)	5,005	(8,637)	(8,239)

Line 21. Operating income.   The result of subtracting line 20 from line 15. In simple terms, this is what the company earned from operations before taxes. The number excludes all investment income.

Operating income may be the most critical line in the entire income statement because it is the hardest to manipulate. Operating income is the pure result of doing business. It does not account for charges such as interest or taxes, which can fluctuate wildly and skew results.

㉒ Other income, principally interest	1,377	1,113	573

Line 22. Other income, principally interest.   Here you learn what a company makes on its investments (cash, bonds, and, sometimes, stocks). That's not a lead headline for IBM, but it can be for some companies.

Do not be impressed by investment income. For one thing, the market pays a low premium for this kind of income. Investment income can help mask losses from continuing operations, which should be the real focus of analysis. Moreover, if the company doesn't make money from operations, it will eventually liquidate its investments in a quest for cash.

In fact, a big jump in investment income may reflect nothing more than a smart one-time investing coup. Better than a loss, surely, but there's no reason to expect that a manufacturing company will replicate this feat year after year. (If a company traditionally makes much of its money from shrewd investments, that's a different story.)

㉓ Interest expense	K	1,227	1,273	1,360

Line 23. Interest expense.   What the company pays each year to service debt. Any significant rise may indicate that the company

has increased its debt load (a glance at the balance sheet will tell you) and should make you wary. Or, it may reflect a general rise in rates. Worse yet, it may indicate that the rates the company pays have risen because its financial situation has worsened.

Note K discusses the amount of IBM's total borrowing, the average interest rate it pays (8% in 1994), and overall reductions in indebtedness. We'll address those numbers when we analyze the balance sheet.

24 Earnings (loss) before income taxes	5,155	(8,797)	(9,026)

Line 24. Earnings before income taxes. The result of adding lines 21 and 22 and then subtracting line 23.

For IBM, this $5.2 billion in pre-tax profit is a stunning swing from the 1993 loss of $8.8 billion. That's a $14 billion difference!

To do an apples-to-apples comparison, back out the restructuring charges as we did in line 15 to see what has really changed. The real pre-tax earnings gain was $5,155 million minus $308 million, or $4.84 billion. Why the huge difference?

According to the chairman's letter, expenses were reduced by $3.5 billion; that accounts for 72% of the turnaround. But profits grew by $1.3 billion without the cost-cutting. The 1994 revenue increase of $1.6 billion might account for some of that, but not much.

We need to understand the other ways IBM's business was improving. To find out, ask the company and analysts what caused the better profit performance. Was it higher prices? A shift to higher-margin products? The declining importance of a division that had been a drag on earnings?

Such information would be important in any case, but it is crucial for IBM because Gerstner says that the 1995 target for cost-cutting is only $1.7 billion—less than half of the $3.5 billion saved in 1994. Even if IBM achieves its stated goal (and not every company does), you should have a sense of where the rest of its profits are going to come from.

| 25 Provision (benefit) for income taxes | H | 2,134 | (810) | (2,161) |

Line 25. Provision (benefit) for income taxes. Yes, corporations pay taxes too. Taxes must be debited from income before calculating an earnings-per-share number.

The word *benefit* in parentheses refers to operating loss carryforwards—previous losses that can be used to lower or eliminate current taxable earnings. Such benefits are extremely valuable for a one-time money loser that has become profitable.

Be forewarned, however, that a money-making company eventually uses up all its tax-loss breaks. When that happens, hefty corporate taxes kick in. Reported earnings may grow more slowly or even decline once the tax losses run out. You cannot talk intelligently about a company unless you know the rate at which its earnings are taxed.

Note H provides almost three full pages of minute detail on tax matters. Don't despair. Only one line is relevant for our assessment of IBM's future earnings. Look at the consolidated income tax rate. It was 24% in 1992, 9% in 1993, and 41% in 1994. Now that the company is solidly profitable, you can assume that the rate will be approximately 41% for 1995 as well.

| 26 Net earnings (loss) before changes in accounting principles | | 3,021 | (7,987) | (6,865) |

Line 26. Net earnings (loss) before changes in accounting principles. The result of subtracting line 25 from line 24.

| 27 Effect of changes in accounting principles | B | – | (114) | 1,900 |

Line 27. Effect of changes in accounting principles. Nothing here for IBM in 1994, but the entry can occasionally be very important. If earnings previously looked shabby, but now, after the impact of fancy new accounting techniques, they look just marvelous, you have to wonder how much of the difference is real.

A change in accounting principles may be a clue that some chicanery is going on. On the other hand, the changes may be thoroughly legitimate. To find out, snoop around. Talk to people at the company and to outside analysts. Read articles and research reports until you know what accounting shifts were made and why. If the information is impossible to get, that's not a good sign. (You can never be certain about the prospects for a stock, but you can learn to avoid this kind of uncertainty.)

Note B states exactly which new accounting methods were adopted for the 1994 statement by IBM; none had an impact on operating results.

28 Net earnings (loss)	3,021	(8,101)	(4,965)

Line 28. Net earnings (loss).   Line 26 minus line 27.

29 Preferred stock dividends	84	47	–

Line 29. Preferred stock dividends.   Few small-cap companies issue preferred stock, but many large corporations do. Preferred stockholders have an advantage over the rest of us, who own common stock. In the event of financial trouble, holders of the preferred get all the dividends due them before common shareholders get a penny in dividends. They may also have an advantage if the company ever liquidates.

As a result, the dividends owed each year to preferred shareholders—$84 million in IBM's case—come right out of the bottom line. This money can never be applicable to common shareholders because it is destined to go elsewhere.

30 Net earnings (loss) applicable to common shareholders	$ 2,937	$(8,148)	$(4,965)

Line 30. Net earnings (loss) applicable to common shareholders.   Net earnings (line 28) minus preferred stock dividends (line 29).

31 *Per share of common stock amounts:*
Before changes in accounting
   principles $ 5.02 $(14.02) $(12.03)

Line 31. Per share of common stock amounts: Before changes in accounting principles. This is what earnings per share would have been according to last year's accounting standards.

32 Effect of changes in accounting
   principles   **B**   –   (.20)   3.33

Line 32. Effect of changes in accounting principles. No change for IBM in 1994.

33 Net earnings (loss) applicable to
   common shareholders $ 5.02 $(14.22) $ (8.70)

Line 33. Net earnings (loss) applicable to common shareholders. This, at last, is the famous earnings-per-share (EPS) number that analysts and investors toss around endlessly. IBM's $5.02 per share (EPS) figure is calculated by dividing net earnings applicable to common shareholders (line 30) by the average number of shares outstanding for the entire year (line 34).

The stock was at $83.00 when the report was issued, so IBM's price-to-earnings (P/E) ratio was 16.5 ($83.00 divided by $5.02). Or, more precisely, 16.5 times trailing twelve-month earnings. Whenever you read about or discuss a stock's P/E multiple, be sure you know whether the number refers to last year's actual earnings or this year's projected earnings.

34 Average number of common shares outstanding
   1994–584,958,699; 1993–573,239,240; 1992–570,896,489

Line 34. Average number of common shares outstanding. You can't calculate earnings per share without this number. But you also need to know whether the amount of stock outstanding is rising or falling—and how steep the trend is.

If the number of shares is declining, the company is most likely buying back some of its own stock. That's almost always good news. It makes sense to repurchase shares only if you think they're undervalued.

In a way, the corporate situation is similar to insider buying by individuals, except that here the insider/buyer is the corporation itself. This type of corporate purchase, however, has a direct impact on earnings per share. Because fewer shares are outstanding after a buyback, the earnings applicable to each common share will be greater.

The number of shares outstanding usually rises for two reasons:

1. The exercise price of stock options, warrants, or convertible debentures is reached. Accountants do not wait for the actual exercise or conversion to occur; they adjust the shares-outstanding number on the assumption that the options are being exercised and turned into actual new shares.

2. The company issues new shares to fund an acquisition or to increase working capital.

When shares increase because of an acquisition, sophisticated investors immediately want to know whether the acquisition will hurt earnings, and for how long. As an example, let's say XYZ earns $10 million a year and has 10 million shares outstanding. It issues 5 million new shares to acquire Eternal Hope Inc. If Eternal Hope earns $5 million, then the acquisition neither helps nor hampers earnings this year. XYZ with 15 million shares will now earn $15 million or $1.00 per share, exactly the same per share as before the acquisition.

If Eternal Hope earns only $4 million, the deal will at least temporarily reduce earnings. XYZ's earnings will fall to $0.93 a share from $1.00. When an acquisition reduces earnings per share, it is said to be dilutive.

As for IBM, the number of shares rose 2.1% from 1993 to 1994 and a minuscule .41% from 1992 to 1993. I'm not thrilled with the trend, but it's nothing to worry about.

THE BALANCE SHEET

The balance sheet is like a snapshot, or an X ray, of a company's financial condition at a particular date. It reveals how a firm is capitalized and provides a tremendous amount of information about what a company's future fortunes might be. Although the balance sheet can't tell you whether new products are selling well, it can give you a clear picture of how a company is managing its debt, accounts receivable, inventories, and other essential items.

As we will soon see, IBM's balance sheet strengthened considerably during 1994.

THE BIG PICTURE

The first part of a balance sheet (the top half, in IBM's case) tabulates total assets. The second part measures corporate liabilities and any dividends payable to shareholders. As I said, this is not so complicated.

In fact, you may be doing the same calculations with your personal or family budget. You start by finding out what you have. Then you determine what you owe. You subtract. What's left over is your net worth. When the same subtraction exercise is performed by a publicly held corporation, the leftover amount is called stockholders' equity. (In some unfortunate cases, it is a negative number.)

Let's walk through the balance sheet line by line, in the same way that we approached the income statement.

Assets

❶ *Current assets:*

Line 1. Current assets. These are assets likely to be converted into cash, or into something of equal value, usually within a year. Lines 2 through 9 are all types of current assets.

CONSOLIDATED STATEMENT OF FINANCIAL POSITION

International Business Machines Corporation and Subsidiary Companies

(Dollars in millions)

At December 31:	Notes	1994	1993
Assets:			
Current assets:			
Cash		$ 1,240	$ 873
Cash equivalents		6,682	4,988
Marketable securities	C	2,632	1,272
Notes and accounts receivable trade, net			
of allowances		14,018	11,676
Sales-type leases receivable		6,351	6,428
Other accounts receivable		1,164	1,308
Inventories	D	6,334	7,565
Prepaid expenses and other current assets		2,917	5,092
Total current assets		41,338	39,202
Plant, rental machines and other property	E	44,820	47,504
Less: Accumulated depreciation		28,156	29,983
Plant, rental machines and other property—net		16,664	17,521
Software, less accumulated amortization			
(1994, $10,793; 1993, $10,143)		2,963	3,703
Investments and sundry assets	F	20,126	20,687
Total assets		$81,091	$81,113
Liabilities and Stockholders' Equity			
Current liabilities:			
Taxes	H	$ 1,771	$ 1,589
Short-term debt	G	9,570	12,097
Accounts payable		3,778	3,400
Compensation and benefits		2,702	2,053
Deferred income		3,475	3,575
Other accrued expenses and liabilities		7,930	10,436
Total current liabilities		29,226	33,150
Long-term debt	G	12,548	15,245
Other liabilities	L	14,023	11,177
Deferred income taxes	H	1,881	1,803
Total liabilities		57,678	61,375
Contingencies	M		
Stockholders' equity:			
Preferred stock, par value $.01 per share—			
shares authorized: 150,000,000			
shares issued: 1994—11,145,000;			
1993—11,250,000	V	1,081	1,091
Common stock, par value $1.25 per share—			
shares authorized: 750,000,000			
shares issues: 1994—588,180,244;			
1993—581,388,475		7,342	6,980
Retained earnings		12,352	10,009
Translation adjustments		2,672	1,658
Treasury stock, at cost (shares: 1994—469,500;			
1993—2,679)		(34)	—
Total stockholders' equity		23,413	19,738
Total liabilities and stockholders' equity		$81,091	$81,113

The notes on pages 52 through 78 are an integral part of this statement.

❷ Cash	$ 1,240	$ 873

Line 2. Cash. Exactly what you think: paper money, coins, money orders, and checks. IBM's $1.2 billion cash hoard isn't huge, but it is up 42% over the previous year—a good trend.

❸ Cash equivalents	6,682	4,988

Line 3. Cash equivalents. To boost investment income, corporations do exactly what you and I do with excess cash. They plant it where it will grow. Common examples of cash equivalents include savings and checking accounts.

IBM's cash equivalents rose 34% in 1994, to $6.7 billion.

❹ Marketable securities	C	2,632	1,272

Line 4. Marketable securities. Usually, government securities and commercial paper (short-term debt issued by corporations). May also include stocks and bonds. These holdings can be either short-term or long-term.

Marketable securities differ from cash equivalents because their liquidation value can vary from day to day.

Note C indicates the breakdown of these securities for IBM: $1 billion in U.S. government securities, $459 million in time deposits and other bank obligations, and $1.2 billion in non-U.S. government securities and other fixed-term obligations.

Before going further, it's smart to add up a company's total cash on hand (lines 2 through 4). For IBM, the figure comes to $10.6 billion. That's a nice chunk of change. By itself, the number means little until you divide it by total shares outstanding. For IBM, the amount is $17.97 per share.

Almost invariably, it is good to see a lot of cash on a balance sheet. If a company's stock trades at $10 and cash on hand equals $5 per share, there's a good chance that the company is undervalued. In fact, it is fair to slash the company's stated P/E ratio by 50% to reflect the excess cash. (Your $10 per share buys the cash for $5 and the rest of the business for the remaining $5.)

Often, cash-rich companies become takeover targets (cash, the ultimate liquid asset, has a way of attracting attention to itself). In any case, excess cash provides a downside cushion for investors, because few companies ever sell for a price lower than the amount of cash on hand per share. Cash can also turn into a cushion if the company's business, or the general economy, goes into a tailspin.

Warning: Cash is not always king. Buckets of cash may be a sign that a profitable company has no interesting opportunities for reinvesting its earnings, or no new product ideas. An ultraconservative company with this approach may not generate impressive stock market returns unless it is taken over, and you can never count on that.

5 Notes and accounts receivable trade, net of allowances	14,018	11,676

Line 5. Notes and accounts receivable—trade, net of allowances. "Notes" here means promissory notes, usually from customers. Accounts receivable are sums owed to the company by customers and others. "Trade, net of allowances" is short for trade receivables (receivables derived from a sale) minus allowances (write-offs for uncollectible debts). Many companies, such as IBM, assume up front that a set percentage of receivables will prove uncollectible.

As revenues rise, the accounts receivable amount normally rises as well. If the growth in accounts receivable significantly outpaces growth in revenues (as it does in IBM's case, 20% versus 2%), you should find out why. Sometimes, the explanation is that the company is allowing customers more time to pay their bills. That's troubling. It means that Company XYZ is giving customers a hidden discount, in the form of interest-free use of money that XYZ should have. This could have a slightly negative impact on earnings and cash flow.

The problems could be even greater. You don't give more generous credit terms to customers when business is booming. Generally, you do it when business has slowed or is slowing, or when many customers lack the resources to pay promptly (another sign that an industry may not be in robust health).

Finally, the accounts receivable amount sometimes increases when there's a problem with a recently shipped product. Customers withhold payment until they're certain that all bugs have been eliminated. Alternately, if a new product is a tough sell, a company may let customers purchase it on a trial basis. The money owed will be paid only when the customer is fully satisfied. A good rule of thumb is that the longer an obligation is outstanding, the less likely that it will ever be paid in full.

6	Sales-type leases receivable	6,351	6,428

Line 6. Sales-type leases receivable. Many companies lease as well as sell their goods. This line indicates expected leasing receivables. If there is a sharp up or down move, you'll want to know why. A big spike in leasing volume may be great for auto companies but dangerous for some technology companies. In a worst-case scenario, the company is having difficulty selling a product rather than leasing it.

The real bad news comes when customers don't renew leases, and the partly outdated products cannot be sold or leased to anyone else. The manufacturer may then realize little, if any, profit on these particular products.

7	Other accounts receivable	1,164	1,308

Line 7. Other accounts receivable. A grab-bag item that's usually of little importance—unless, of course, you notice a dramatic change. In that case, do some more research to find out what is happening and why.

⑧ Inventories	D	6,334	7,565

Line 8. Inventories.   The value of a firm's finished goods, plus raw materials, work in progress, and supplies used to make products.

The trend for IBM is encouraging. In 1994, inventories dropped to $6.3 billion (from $7.6 billion in 1993). When sales are rising (as they were for IBM), such a decline is quite good to see. It shows that the company is using its capital more efficiently.

Rising inventory levels are sometimes a red flag, but not always. If sales are growing quickly, inventories often rise as well. The trend becomes disturbing when inventories are rising more rapidly than revenues.

Note D breaks out total inventories into three groups: (1) finished goods, (2) work in process, and (3) raw materials.

⑨ Prepaid expenses and other current assets	2,917	5,092

Line 9. Prepaid expenses and other current assets.   The household model applies here. Prepaid expenses are amounts paid in advance of the period they cover. For a family, the most common prepaid outlay would be insurance, especially if payments are made once a year. For a corporation, prepaid expenses typically include insurance, rent, advertising, interest, and supplies.

⑩ Total current assets	41,338	39,202

Line 10. Total current assets.   The sum of lines 2 through 9.

⑪ Plant, rental machines and other property	E	44,820	47,504

Line 11. Plant, rental machines, and other property.   In standard accounting, such assets are listed at cost rather than at today's estimated value. Sometimes, this creates opportunities for bargain hunters. Any company with large, undeveloped land holdings will be worth more than this line item suggests. If some of the land is

in a great place, the company might someday realize a windfall not accurately reflected on its balance sheet.

Note E divides this category into land and land improvements; buildings; plant, laboratory, and office equipment; and rental machines and parts.

⑫ Less: Accumulated depreciation		28,156	29,983

Line 12. Less: Accumulated depreciation. Accumulated depreciation is the sum of all depreciation taken to date on items that are still recognized as corporate assets.

⑬ Plant, rental machines and other property—net		16,664	17,521

Line 13. Plant, rental machines, and other property—net. Line 11 minus line 12.

⑭ Software, less accumulated amortization (1994, $10,793; 1993, $10,143)		2,963	3,703

Line 14. Software, less accumulated amortization. Like line 12.

⑮ Investments and sundry assets	F	20,126	20,687

Line 15. Investments and sundry assets. This will cover different items for every company. For IBM, the details are spelled out in note F. The major item is investment in sales-type leases. Translation: This is the value of the equipment that IBM leases to customers.

Other items are deferred taxes (see line 27 for explanation), prepaid pension cost, noncurrent customer loan receivables (debts that IBM has not written off and expects to receive eventually), installment payment receivables, investments in business alliances, goodwill, and other investments and sundry assets.

⑯ Total assets		$81,091	$81,113

Line 16. Total assets.   The sum of lines 10, 13, and 15. Note that IBM's assets are down slightly from 1993. By itself that's not worrisome, until you compare it to the total of liabilities. When a company is using a lot of excess cash to pay down debt—which IBM did in 1994—total assets may remain flat or decline. But if liabilities are shrinking significantly, the actual value of the business will be higher.

Liabilities and Stockholders' Equity

A liability—the opposite of an asset—is an obligation to pay money or deliver goods and services.

⑰ Current liabilities:			

Line 17. Current liabilities.   Generally, these are obligations that are expected to be met within twelve months.

⑱ Taxes	H	$ 1,771	$ 1,589

Line 18. Taxes.   Like self-employed individuals, corporations make periodic tax payments based on income estimates. This line item refers to the amount of taxes, domestic and foreign, that IBM owes at the moment.

Note H, mentioned in the income statement discussion, provides more details.

⑲ Short-term debt	G	9,570	12,097

Line 19. Short-term debt.   Debt due within a year, including commercial paper, short-term loans, and the portion of long-term debt that must be paid during the next twelve months.

Note G provides segment breakdowns of the debt and states the average rates IBM is paying, as of December 31, 1994, for commercial paper (4.9%) and short-term loans (6.6%).

For some companies, especially small ones, the amount of debt can mean the difference between life and death. A company's products may be great, but if debt is overwhelming, the company may go bankrupt before its products have enough time to earn a marketplace niche.

This is an extremely important item for our IBM analysis because the company slashed short-term debt by a remarkable $2.5 billion, or 21%, in 1994. In fact, debt reduction, perhaps more than anything else, is what has left IBM with a far stronger balance sheet in 1994 than in 1993.

20 Accounts payable	3,778	3,400

Line 20. Accounts payable. Debts incurred primarily to purchase supplies, inventory, and services. The numbers are fairly small considering IBM's size, so I'm not concerned that accounts payable rose 11% in 1994.

21 Compensation and benefits	2,702	2,053

Line 21. Compensation and benefits. Includes payments owed to employees and, sometimes, payroll-related taxes (such as employee income taxes and social security taxes that have been withheld).

The growth of this line item was jolting in percentage terms (up 32%) but not particularly important in actual dollars ($649 million).

22 Deferred income	3,475	3,575

Line 22. Deferred income. Also known as unearned revenues or unearned income, this is income received or recorded before it is earned. Why is it a liability? Because IBM must now either deliver a

product or service, or offer a total refund. Relevant examples for IBM would be lease rentals or advance repair service contracts.

For IBM, there was hardly any year-to-year change.

23	Other accrued expenses and liabilities	7,930	10,436

Line 23. Other accrued expenses and liabilities.   These are payments that may not be due for quite a while, although standard accounting principles require that they be expensed as incurred.

Note the $2.5 billion drop for IBM. It's another sign that the company is reining in liabilities.

24	Total current liabilities	29,226	33,150

Line 24. Total current liabilities.   The sum of lines 18 through 23.

IBM's total current liabilities dropped by $3.9 billion, or 12%, in 1994. A great performance, and one of the reasons IBM's balance sheet has become more solid. The company is much less risky than it was a year ago.

How can you tell? Calculate the current and quick ratios. The current ratio is total current assets (line 10) divided by total current liabilities (line 24). It assesses a company's ability to meet current obligations with assets on hand. For IBM, the ratio is 1.41, which is very healthy (a number under 1 should raise a flag).

The quick ratio is identical, with one important exception. Inventory is not counted as an asset because it can take a long time to convert some products and supplies into cash, and because their value may have declined over time. A warehouse full of three-year-old PCs isn't worth the one-time list price nor is it worth the cost of manufacturing. The hoard might draw some money at a scrap sale, if the owner is lucky.

A warehouse stocked with Coca-Cola syrup or Gillette Sensor razor blades is worth real money. The quick ratio penalizes companies whose inventory can be easily sold. In fact, the faster the inventory turns over (Coke syrup moves faster than Caterpillar bull-dozers), the lower the quick ratio can be without causing alarm. I like to see a quick ratio of 1 or higher. IBM's quick ratio is 1.2, which is just fine.

25 Long-term debt	G	12,548	15,245

Line 25. Long-term debt. Typically, debt that is to be paid in twelve months or over a longer period.

Note G reveals the years in which different amounts of debt are due and the currencies in which debts are held ($4.769 billion of Japanese yen-denominated debt was to come due from 1995 to 2014, for example).

26 Other liabilities	L	14,023	11,177

Line 26. Other liabilities. Almost anything can fit here.

Note L says that, for IBM, this includes costs for environmental cleanup at operating facilities, previously owned facilities, and Superfund sites. Most of these "other liabilities," however, are for non-pension postretirement benefits, indemnity, and retirement plan reserves for non-U.S. employees. The category also includes some restructuring charges.

27 Deferred income taxes	H	1,881	1,803

Line 27. Deferred income taxes. This item arises because corporations keep at least two sets of books, one for accounting purposes and one for the IRS.

Let's say a company buys an asset for $1,000. For tax purposes, it takes advantage of accelerated depreciation by writing off $200 during the asset's first year. For accounting purposes, however, such items are almost always depreciated using the straight-line method (prorating depreciation over the expected life of the asset). If the expected life is 10 years, the company would write off $100 in the first year.

What if the company sold the item for $1,000 after one year? It would have a tax liability of $200 rather than $100. The deferred income tax item recognizes this potential tax liability. (Many analysts back this item out because they assume that a new IBM notebook computer manufacturing facility will not be sold during its productive life. So the deferred taxes will never have to be paid.)

Note: Deferred taxes will be listed as an asset, rather than a liability, when items are written off more quickly for accounting purposes than for tax purposes.

Note readers will uncover an interesting nugget in note H. IBM still has $4 billion in tax credit carry-forwards to offset future income. In other words, now that IBM is earning money again, it can apply these old losses to its tax bill, thus lowering the size of its tax burden for future, profitable quarters.

28	Total liabilities	57,678	61,375

Line 28. Total liabilities.   The sum of lines 24 through 27. It is often distressing when a company makes major cuts in current liabilities only to take on more long-term debt and other long-term liabilities. That smacks of refinancing rather than debt reduction. Furthermore, long-term debt is much more expensive than short-term obligations.

Happily, IBM doesn't have this problem. Current liabilities fell $3.9 billion in 1994, and total liabilities dropped $3.7 billion, almost as much.

29	Contingencies	M

Line 29. Contingencies.   Money set aside to cover pending litigation, class-action lawsuit expenses, bad loans, or other business misadventures. We learn from note M that, in 1993, shareholders brought a class-action complaint that remains unsettled. In the note, IBM says its defense is strong and the case will have no material impact on the company's earnings or financial condition.

30 Stockholders' equity:

Line 30. Stockholders' equity.   The owners' equity in a corporation. It has two main sources: (1) investments made directly by shareholders (called paid-in capital) and (2) profits kept by the business (called retained earnings).

Watch the trend. At a successful company, stockholders' equity should climb year after year. IBM wasn't a successful company in the early 1990s. Immense write-offs lowered stockholders' equity in 1992 and 1993. But 1994 reversed the trend, and I think further gains lie ahead.

31 Preferred stock, par value $.01 per share— shares authorized: 150,000,000 shares issued: 1994—11,145,000; 1993—11,250,000	V	1,081	1,091

Line 31. Preferred stock.   See the discussion of line 28 of the income statement.

Note: Par value means a lot for a bond—it tells you what the bond can be redeemed for upon maturity—but it is virtually meaningless for preferred and common stock. Par value is an arbitrary amount chosen by the stock issuer. It does not set a floor price above which a stock must trade. Trust me, I know this firsthand.

Shares authorized is the total number of shares of a class of stock that can be issued by a corporation. The board of directors sets the number.

Note V points out that on June 7, 1993, IBM issued 11.25 million shares of Series A preferred stock.

32 Common stock, par value $1.25 per share— shares authorized: 750,000,000 shares issues: 1994—588,180,244; 1993—581,388,475	7,342	6,980

Line 32. Common stock.   If you're checking the numbers closely, you may notice a discrepancy. Here it says that IBM

had 588,180,244 shares outstanding in 1994. The number used for the income statement was 584,958,699, about 3.5 million fewer shares.

The explanation is simple. To calculate earnings per share, you divide earnings by the average number of shares outstanding for the entire year (584,958,699). But the balance sheet is a snapshot on a specific day, so the number used there is the shares outstanding on December 31, 1994 (588,180,244).

㉝	Retained earnings	12,352	10,009

Line 33. Retained earnings. Net profits kept by a corporation after dividends are paid. This is a cumulative number, reflecting all profits ever retained. Annual losses are subtracted from retained earnings.

In 1994, IBM's retained earnings soared 23%, an excellent performance for a huge company.

㉞	Translation adjustments	2,672	1,658

Line 34. Translation adjustments. This reflects gains or losses from foreign currency translations. The U.S. dollar weakened throughout 1994, causing most U.S.-based multinational corporations to report positive currency swings for the year. IBM made $2.7 billion in 1994 because so much of its business is international.

However, this is one instance when an existing trend may have little meaning for an investor, unless he or she is a currency expert. In fact, a huge currency translation gain can be a red flag. There's no reason to expect such gains to continue. The amount should be factored out when you analyze a company's growth rate. Example: If 20% of a company's earnings came from currency gains and its earnings grew 20%, you don't have a 20% grower. You have a company that's stalled—and may be heading nowhere.

35 Treasury stock, at cost (shares: 1994—469,500;
    1993—2,679)   (34)   —

Line 35. Treasury stock, at cost. A minor matter. This refers to stock, common or preferred, issued by the corporation and then reacquired for certain needs (such as a stock bonus plan for managers and employees).

36 Total stockholders' equity   23,413   19,738

Line 36. Total stockholders' equity. The sum of lines 32 through 35. This is also sometimes called book value per share, which can mislead you if you're not careful.

Book value is an important analytical tool when you're looking at financial stocks, such as banks, investment bankers, and insurance companies. It is also useful if you're dissecting companies with a huge amount of cash on hand. But, for a high-tech or cutting-edge manufacturing company, book value may be worth only a brief look—in part because the most valuable assets a technology company has are intangible things like a bold new patent or a dominant market share.

All things being equal, though, I'd prefer to buy a company selling for two times book value rather than nine times book value. In some cases, book value can help set a floor for a stock.

That's little comfort with IBM. IBM's book value is $39.80 per share. So, at $83 per share, it is selling for 2.09 times book value. Therefore, the market capitalization of IBM (stock price multiplied by shares outstanding) is more than twice the company's book value, or $48.8 billion.

Why isn't stockholders' equity listed on the asset side of the ledger? Because the corporation doesn't own the equity. The equity belongs to shareholders. If IBM were liquidated tomorrow, everything left over after paying creditors would have to be distributed to shareholders.

One measure I like to use to assess the financial stability of a company is its debt-to-equity ratio. To get it, divide total long-term debt by total shareholders' equity. For IBM, the number is 53.6%.

That's high compared to competitors such as Hewlett-Packard—indeed, it's about 10% higher than the average large computer company—but I can live with it. Besides, the trend is positive. In 1993, the number was 77.2%. That's a huge change in one year.

When looking at a company's debt structure, cash flow analysis (see below) can be crucial. If I see annual cash flow that is sharply higher than the annual interest on the company's debt, I relax a little. If the cash flow is insufficient to cover the debt, I think twice before buying the stock. In this case, I need a very strong reason to believe that the cash flow picture will change, and that the change will happen soon.

The higher a company's debt-to-equity ratio, the more important cash flow becomes. That's because strong cash flow provides safety. Weak cash flow, more often than not, is an invitation to disaster.

Another crucial measure of corporate performance is return on equity (ROE), calculated by dividing total earnings by total shareholders' equity. The result reveals how efficiently management is using its resources to generate profits.

ROE percentages differ among industries, so be careful when you're using ROE as a measure to help pick stocks. Technology companies, for example, usually have a much higher ROE than companies in smokestack industries. For technology companies, I am attracted by an ROE of 15% or more. The higher the ROE number, the higher the P/E multiple can be.

IBM's return on equity in 1994 is line 30 of the income statement ($2.937 billion) divided by line 36 of the balance sheet ($23.413 billion) minus line 31 of the balance sheet ($1.081 billion, the liquidation value of the preferred stock). IBM's ROE is 13%. That's low for computer companies but above the 9.95% hurdle rate to make a stock an appealing investment.

Hurdle rate (which changes often) is calculated by adding the following percentages:

6.30%   The interest rate on 30-year U.S. Treasury bonds

2.60%   The Consumer Price Index inflation rate for the past year

1.05%   The beta of the stock in question (a beta of more than 1 means a stock is more volatile than the overall market; a beta below 1 means it is less volatile)

The total in this case is 9.95%. IBM's return on equity exceeds the hurdle rate by three percentage points, another reason not to consider IBM stodgy and over the hill.

37 Total liabilities and stockholders' equity	$81,091	$81,113

Line 37. Total liabilities and stockholders' equity. Line 28 plus line 36.

Compare this amount to the total assets figure in line 16. They're identical, as they will be for every corporation. A balance sheet is always balanced.

CASH FLOW STATEMENT

"Profits are an opinion, but cash is a fact." That old saw represents the view of many financial experts. For the most part, it's a sound notion to follow.

The cash flow statement can be enormously valuable. Unfortunately, not enough investors pay close attention to it. By looking at cash flow, you can determine how well management is using company assets, as well as where cash is coming from and where it is going.

The cash flow statement is relatively free from accounting gimmickry. Profits, which show up on the income statement, are an "opinion" because they can be massaged or managed. They do not represent Truth with a capital "T."

The cash flow statement is much more straightforward. In many industries, cash flow rather than earnings constitutes the real bottom line. Industries in which earnings are all but irrelevant include broadcasting, cable television, and leasing companies, among others.

Cash flow, alas, isn't a perfect analytic tool. It is most appropriate for media and real estate enterprises that have to make large initial investments (in plant, equipment, or land) but much smaller ones later on.

For manufacturers such as IBM, cash flow analysis says *something* about value but not everything. You can't predict what capital improvements and investments IBM will have to make in the near future to keep pace with competitors. It's best to analyze cash flow only after subtracting expected capital expenditures for next year, the year after, and the year after that.

What if the cash is flowing the wrong way—out rather than in? Negative cash flow should not necessarily be alarming. In fact, it is quite common among young or development-stage companies. For small biotech concerns, it is practically inevitable. At a mature company, however, negative cash flow can be terrible news.

In 1984, negative cash flow led me to short a 100-year-old company listed on the New York Stock Exchange. The dinosaur in question was Western Union.

Based on the stock price, investors seemed to be ignoring the fact that cash flow had been unable to cover capital spending for five consecutive years. Western Union was spending a fortune on new equipment and new ventures, but had nothing to show for its investments. And its established businesses were doing little to pick up the slack.

I wouldn't have shorted the stock if I had believed that any of the company's new ventures looked promising. But none of them looked good to me. My diagnosis was that Western Union was a company whose core business was under pressure from competitors and new technology, and whose effort to diversify had been a flop. That's the perfect recipe for a declining stock.

So I shorted it, and it became one of my most successful short sales. Western Union eventually declared bankruptcy and the stock went much lower. I was able to profit from the disaster because I paid

CONSOLIDATED STATEMENT OF CASH FLOWS

International Business Machines Corporation and Subsidiary Companies

(Dollars in millions)

For the year ended December 31:	1994	1993	1992
Cash flow from operating activities:			
Net earnings (loss)	$ 3,021	$(8,101)	$ (4,965)
Adjustments to reconcile net earnings (loss) to cash provided from operating activities:			
Effect of changes in accounting principles	—	114	(1,900)
Effect of restructuring charges	(2,772)	5,230	8,312
Depreciation	4,197	4,710	4,793
Deferred income taxes	825	(1,335)	(3,356)
Amortization of software	2,098	1,951	1,466
(Gain) loss on disposition of investment assets	(11)	151	54
Other changes that provided (used) cash:			
Receivables	653	1,185	1,052
Inventories	1,518	583	704
Other assets	187	1,865	110
Accounts payable	305	359	(311)
Other liabilities	1,772	1,615	315
Net cash provided from operating activities	11,793	8,327	6,274
Cash flow from investing activities:			
Payments for plant, rental machines and other property	(3,078)	(3,154)	(4,751)
Proceeds from disposition of plant, rental machines and other property	900	793	633
Investment in software	(1,361)	(1,507)	(1,752)
Purchases of marketable securities and other investments	(3,866)	(2,721)	(3,284)
Proceeds from marketable securities and other investments	2,476	2,387	3,276
Proceeds from the sale of Federal Systems Company	1,503	—	—
Net cash used in investing activities	(3,426)	(4,202)	(5,878)
Cash flow from financing activities:			
Proceeds from new debt	5,335	11,794	10,045
Payments to settle debt	(9,445)	(8,741)	(10,735)
Short-term borrowings less than 90 days-net	(1,948)	(5,247)	4,199
Preferred stock transactions-net	(10)	1,091	—
Common stock transactions-net	318	122	(90)
Cash dividends paid	(662)	(933)	(2,765)
Net cash (used in) provided from financing activities	(6,412)	(1,914)	654
Effect of exchange rate changes on cash and cash equivalents	106	(796)	(549)
Net change in cash and cash equivalents	2,061	1,415	501
Cash and cash equivalents at January 1	5,861	4,446	3,945
Cash and cash equivalents at December 31	$ 7,922	$ 5,861	$ 4,446
Supplemental data:			
Cash paid during the year for:			
Income taxes	$ 287	$ 452	$ 1,297
Interest	$ 2,132	$ 2,410	$ 3,132

The notes on pages 52 through 78 are an integral part of this statement.

attention to the fact that Western Union was blowing through its cash without any sound business plan to regenerate it.

The cash flow statement is divided into three parts: (1) cash flow from operating activities, (2) cash flow from investing activities, and (3) cash flow from financing activities. The first section—cash flow from operating activities—is far more significant than the other two. The big question, as always, is: What's the trend?

Let's look at the key lines in the cash flow statement.

❻ Depreciation	4,197	4,710	4,793

Line 6. Depreciation. Depreciation penalizes earnings on the income statement, but it doesn't take cash out of a company's pocket. (You have the same advantage on your tax return, when you depreciate a house, a computer, or other qualifying purchase.) The depreciation line contributes $4.197 billion to IBM's operating cash flow.

❽ Amortization of software	2,098	1,951	1,466

Line 8. Amortization of software. Amortization, like depreciation, is an operating expense that does not require a cash outflow.

⓰ Net cash provided from operating activities	11,793	8,327	6,274

Line 16. Net cash provided from operating activities. This line, the key item in any cash flow statement, illustrates the critical trend for IBM. In 1994, net cash flow from operations was 88% higher than it was just two years earlier. Nearly doubling cash flow in two years is a phenomenal performance.

To determine how the stock market values this cash flow, divide $11.793 billion into the market value of IBM ($48 billion at the time we were looking at it). The answer is 4.01, which means that, at a price of $83 per share, IBM stock is trading for 4.01 times operating cash flow. That's very cheap, and it makes the stock more attractive.

That low multiple also reflects uncertainty about IBM's future cash-generating power.

17 Cash flow from investing activities:

Line 17. Cash flow from investing activities. Companies can obtain cash from investing as well as from operations.

21 Purchases of marketable securities and
other investments   (3,866)   (2,721)   (3,284)

Line 21. Purchases of marketable securities and other investments. When a company buys bonds, stocks, or other securities, cash flow suffers—even if the value of the holdings rises rather than falls. This is one of the reasons analysts usually value a company according to its operating cash flow, eliminating figures from investing and financing activities.

22 Proceeds from marketable securities and
other investments   2,476   2,387   3,276

Line 22. Proceeds from marketable securities and other investments. When bonds, stocks, or other investments are sold, cash flow rises. Again, this kind of improvement in cash flow is wholly or partly illusory.

23 Proceeds from the sale of Federal Systems
Company   1,503   —   —

Line 23. Proceeds from the sale of Federal Systems Company. Asset sales also boost cash flow. IBM's sale of Federal Systems in 1994 is a good example. (The same transaction served to lower net earnings, because of the write-off involved. On the cash flow statement, we see an upside: the money that IBM raised from selling off the subsidiary.)

㉕ Cash flow from financing activities:

Line 25. Cash flow from financing activities.   Financing activities typically affect a company's long-term capital needs. A company can obtain cash by issuing stock or by long-term borrowing. Cash flow will decline when a company repurchases its own stock, repays loans, and pays cash dividends.

㉖ Proceeds from new debt	5,335	11,794	10,045

Line 26. Proceeds from new debt.   New borrowing is sharply lower for IBM: in 1994, it fell $6.459 billion, or 55%, to $5.335 billion. Great news for IBM's balance sheet, but not for cash flow.

㉗ Payments to settle debt	(9,445)	(8,741)	(10,735)

Line 27. Payments to settle debt.   Paying down debt is great, despite the fact that it has a negative impact on cash flow.

㉛ Cash dividends paid	(662)	(933)	(2,765)

Line 31. Cash dividends paid.   In 1994, IBM paid out $2.103 billion less in dividends than it did in 1992. The explanation isn't mysterious. In 1992, IBM cut its common stock dividend.

SUMMARY OF IBM'S FINANCIAL STATEMENTS

IBM, in 1994, had gotten religion about reinventing itself. The new IBM was anything but complacent. Management had shown its ability and determination to make extraordinary cost reductions.

Cost-cutting was responsible for about two-thirds of the profits reported in 1994. Intelligent cost-cutting can be a boon to shareholders, but it can last only so long. Just as earnings cannot grow to the sky, costs cannot fall through the floor. There is a finite number of people you can lay off and plants you can close.

Nonetheless, IBM's new cost structure meant that making large profits was now much easier than it had been three years earlier, when the Gerstner regime began.

The central message conveyed in the 1994 annual report is that IBM is no dinosaur. Despite the downsizing, it remains a forward-looking company. Its 1994 R&D budget alone was greater than Microsoft's total revenue base for the same year—and Microsoft is considered a research titan.

These statements profile a company invigorated by new management and positioned in an increasingly powerful financial situation. Reading the annual report, I concluded that IBM's stock had some more room to move in the near future.

FINANCIAL FUNNY BUSINESS

If a company's management is determined to cook the books, even the most sophisticated investors may be snookered. A clear-eyed look at a company's accounting practices can help you avoid stocks whose prices are being inflated by legal, but irresponsible, accounting gimmicks.

Which brings us to the story of Future Healthcare. The Cincinnati-based company, which conducts clinical trials for pharmaceutical firms, had a terrific PEG ratio: .5. (The PEG ratio is the P/E ratio divided by the company's expected growth rate.) And there were many other reasons why the stock was appealing; for example:

- In June 1994, Future Healthcare reported a quarterly earnings gain of 400%, to $0.10 a share.

- The pharmaceutical testing market was huge—$11 billion—and growing fast.

- Future Healthcare was winning more than 95% of the contracts on which it bid.

- The company's overall selling, general, and administrative (SG&A) expenses were declining during a period of rapid growth, allowing it to bring a greater percentage of revenue to the bottom line.

We recommended the stock at $11.75 in July 1994. Eight months later, we were all smiles as it soared to $24, a gain of 104%. When I last checked, you could buy Future Healthcare for $4.06.

What happened? We and many other investors didn't do our homework well enough. In the summer of 1994, the first hint that something might be wrong appeared, and we missed it.

Nothing seemed problematic about the stock or analysts' opinions about the future. Future Healthcare was trading at six times its October 1992 initial public offering (IPO) price, and its recently released 1993 form 10-K seemed a picture of health. The year's sales had doubled to $10.3 million, and earnings almost tripled, from $0.11 to $0.29 per share. Analysts' consensus was that earnings would rise 72% in 1994, to $0.50 a share.

The company's income statement looked great. Future's cash flow statement, however, told a very different story. In 1993 alone, the company lost nearly $5 million on operations. Were it not for a $5.5 million debt offering, Future Healthcare would have been unable to pay its bills. Someone who might have probed deeply could have learned, in mid-1994, that the discrepancy between cash flow and income lay in the way the company recognized revenue.

Future's testing business was a slow-moving operation. Tests took a long time—about four or five months for developing guidelines, and another nine to twelve months for actual testing. That's a total of thirteen to seventeen months per project. Future would usually get 10% to 25% of its fees up front, to begin enrolling patients. The company would not send another bill to the test sponsor until the test reached a predetermined milestone—usually, a third of the way through, or three to four months into a test.

Some testing companies recognize revenue when they bill the sponsor. More conservative outfits book revenue when they get paid.

Future took an entirely different approach. Using what might be called "pathologically aggressive accounting," Future recognized revenues as soon as initial patient visits were conducted. In other words, three to six months before even sending a bill to sponsors, Future was already chalking up sales for its work. The actual cash generated by those sales might not arrive at Future headquarters for nine months or more.

It is highly unusual to recognize revenue before billing. By booking sales so prematurely, Future was counting on some revenue it would never get. Booking a sale as a patient enters a test is especially misleading in Future's kind of business. Some subjects invariably drop out of tests, and drug companies often do not pay for such dropouts.

Nathan Messenger, a vice president at Collaborative Clinical Research, a Future competitor, says, "What they call revenue is not reality." Calls to Messenger and other Future competitors might have helped investors avoid the debacle.

When you see a questionable accounting practice, it is vital that you find out how significant the technique's impact really is. In the case of IBM, my only accounting objection—to the capitalization of some software development—amounted to a quibble. The accounting decision did not dramatically change IBM's bottom line.

It sure did at Future. Of the $9.3 million reported as revenues in Future's 1993 form 10-K, about $6.2 million—or fully two-thirds of it—had not yet been billed! That's terrible, but the story gets even worse.

While it was overstating revenues, Future was also understating expenses. The company typically spent large sums on advertising, recruiting, and patient screening for each clinical trial. Instead of expensing those costs as occurred, Future capitalized them and wrote them off over the life of the contract. These expenses contributed to the company's cash drain. In the 1993 form 10-K, Future showed that it capitalized $2.1 million in expenses under "contracts in progress."

The problem created was twofold. First, Future could not assume that it would ever get paid for this groundwork. Drug companies sometimes curtail trials in midstream, paying some costs and sticking testers with others.

Second, and more important, few of Future's competitors capitalize costs. When you come upon a questionable accounting practice, it is always smart to check out what competitors are doing in similar situations. It's an easy process because the competitors are filing the same financial documents and resolving the same types of questions. Just compare and contrast.

In fairness, Future's action was partly defensive. An ominous industry trend had emerged: Clients such as Merck were delaying payment until later in the testing process. That's legitimate bad news, precisely the kind an investor is entitled to know. It's not a fact to be papered over with questionable accounting.

By the time Future released its September 1994 nine-month earnings, capitalized startup costs had almost doubled to $4.1 billion. Accounts receivable rose to $15.3 million, higher than the company's $14.4 million in revenues for the same period. Of the $15.3 million in receivables, $10.3 million—or 67%—was unbilled.

During the first nine months of 1994, Future's cash flow was a negative $2.1 million. Remember, that means more money is going out of the firm than is coming in, and at some point a well like that runs dry. To cover its expenses during this period, Future tapped the equity market by issuing additional stock. Another $9.7 million was raised. Few, if any, buyers of the stock knew how desperately their funds were needed.

As I indicated earlier, negative cash flow isn't *necessarily* the kiss of death for young companies. But when a stock has quintupled in less than two years, investors should be concerned about a company that is still cash-flow-negative.

If Future had used conservative accounting, all its earnings would have disappeared. The company would have been forced to report a large loss. As it happens, Future's accounting policies were laid out in public documents. Why weren't some smart investors scared away? Possibly because the 1993 form 10-K had the full approval of Big Six accounting giant Price Waterhouse.

Investors love to see a Big Six signature. So, apparently, did Future. The company started with Ernst & Young and switched to KPMG Peat Marwick before signing on with Price Waterhouse.

In February 1994, as KPMG Peat Marwick was gearing up for its annual audit, Future fired the firm. Future says the dismissal was because of costs, but the timing was certainly suspicious. When Price Waterhouse was brought in, it had just a month to complete its audit.

A shift in accountants is always worrisome. In Future's case, however, such shifts were becoming habitual. This kind of turnover among accountants is a flaming red flag.

While analyzing Future's numbers early in 1995, Price Waterhouse came across a disturbing fact. Not all of Future's unbilled receivables were truly receivable. As the auditor began probing customers, Future president Timothy Ross dropped a bombshell: He admitted to inflating revenues for the previous three years.

When Future and the accountants disagreed about what to do next, Future fired Price Waterhouse. The next day, the stock crashed, losing more than half its value.

Investors have filed lawsuits, of course. We don't know how much of the disaster was caused by fraud and how much resulted from extraordinarily shoddy accounting practices. In one sense, it almost doesn't matter. The stated numbers were enough to make investors look elsewhere for a bargain.

The four analysts who regularly followed the company remained bullish until the bad news was splashed all over the business pages. Why so long? One reason is that analysts tend to get too close to a company. If their brokerage firm does investment banking business with the company, this gives them a clear conflict of interest. (Calling a company a ticking time bomb usually causes the CEO to look elsewhere for the next offering of equity or debt.)

Furthermore, Wall Street doesn't like yelling "Sell!" Analysts can get in trouble for saying the word. Long ago, Wall Street learned that "Buy!" was better for business. After all, everyone can buy a recommended stock and give the brokerage firm a commission.

THE SEVEN DEADLIEST SINS

Howard Shilit, author of *Financial Shenanigans*, cites 52 techniques for finding out that a company may not be as sound as its stated financials suggest. Let's focus on the top seven.

1. *A shift to a more aggressive accounting policy.* This may be absolutely legitimate, but, much of the time, management is trying to cover up an earnings shortfall. Beware of any company that decides to amortize goodwill more slowly than originally intended.

2. *Depreciation over a very long period of time.* If a piece of equipment is expected to last ten years, it should be depreciated over ten years, if not faster. It is legal, however, to depreciate an item over twenty or thirty years. The result: A company unrealistically gooses up earnings in the short run while penalizing them in the long run. This is garden-variety sleight of hand, but it often succeeds in misleading investors. (Conservative companies depreciate assets quickly.)

3. *The abrupt resignation or firing of an auditor and/or law firm.* When auditors are dismissed or resign, it is almost invariably a very bad sign. If the change in auditors is announced at about the same time as bad corporate news, you should probably bail out immediately.

   When a Big Six accounting firm is replaced by a firm you've never heard of, it is an even better idea to head for the hills. Sometimes, management really is thinking, "We couldn't fool Ernst & Young, but we may be able to sneak some things past a group of nonentities."

4. *A qualified opinion from an auditor.* Not quite as bad as a resignation, but nonetheless very troubling. It means that the accounting firm either was not given enough information to

stand behind the numbers wholeheartedly, or else had reservations about the accounting methods chosen by management.

It could also mean the accountants disagreed with some statements in the report, or were concerned that some event beyond management's control—such as a pending lawsuit—could have a devastating impact on the company.

5. *One-time gains from the sale of undervalued investments, including real estate.* Such gains should absolutely not be recorded as part of operating earnings. If they are, the company is trying to inflate earnings, which means it is paying more attention to market perception than to shareholders' long-term interests.

6. *The capitalization of start-up, advertising, or research and development costs.* When a company capitalizes costs such as advertising, or research and development, it is usually trying to pull a fast one. (A capitalized cost is deducted from income over time, rather than all at once when the cost is incurred). Even though this year's marketing effort may have some long-term benefits, it is ridiculous to defer the marketing expenses into next year and the year after.

   Watch your wallet when a company begins to defer expenses. The situation is even worse if the deferred expense category is growing faster than revenues.

7. *Hiding losses as "noncontinuing."* Stockpickers are much more troubled by losses from continuing operations than by those at a division that has since been jettisoned. As you look forward, those noncontinuing losses quickly become ancient history. Knowing that investors prefer such losses, some companies try to give them exactly what they seem to want. Except that the losses are really from ongoing operations.

   They won't be ancient history next year. Instead, they will make a return appearance, unless the company is lucky enough to stop the red ink.

3

Earnings

Investors use literally dozens of different strategies to find promising companies. For all their variety, however, one theme is central to all of them: The ultimate goal of a successful investor is to uncover stocks whose earning power is greater than the price of the shares. In short, the name of the game in investing is the bottom line. The bigger it is, the more you can win.

That may sound simple, perhaps even obvious. Nevertheless, too many investors behave as if earnings are an afterthought to the investing process. How so?

When the typical intelligent investor encounters a company whose earnings are growing at 100% a year—or 200% or 400%—he or she naturally thinks, "You can't fool me. This can't possibly last. Trees don't grow to the sky."

In the long run, this hypothetical investor is correct. Triple-digit earnings growth is just a phase. Rapid earnings growth, however, is not always fleeting. And those who act as if it is run the risk of missing out on the biggest opportunities in investing.

Believe it or not, there's a huge group of investors who systematically avoid companies that are reporting explosive earnings gains. These investors are ultimately settling for second-rate returns in the stock market. The truth is, outrageous earnings gains are sustainable for longer than the typical investor thinks. The key is to determine the difference between companies that have lasting earnings growth potential and companies that do not.

To employ this strategy successfully, find out about such companies relatively early in their fast-growth cycle.

Where do you look? Actually, this vital information is readily available and inexpensive. One way to get it is to wade through the entire daily list of reported earnings in *The Wall Street Journal*, looking for the gems. That's not impossibly hard, but there are two much more efficient approaches.

For a better daily list, look at *Investor's Business Daily*, a newspaper that has great earnings coverage. Each day, it prints tables of the companies reporting the biggest quarterly earnings increases (20% or better) and those reporting the biggest declines (negative 20% or worse).

If you prefer to track earnings on a monthly basis, the best source is our magazine, *Individual Investor*. In every issue, we run a five- or six-page section called "America's Fastest Growing Companies" (AFGC), which highlights all companies reporting at least a 100% increase in quarterly earnings during the past month. Those earnings box scores (which include phone numbers so you can contact the companies for more information) are a wonderful source of new investment ideas.

Let me back that statement up with statistics. We've done our own in-house analysis of the performance of the section, and the results may surprise you.

If you had indiscriminately purchased every stock mentioned in the AFGC section in 1993 and had held all of them through the end of 1994, the total return on your investment would have been better than 30%. Had you held the S&P 500 for the entire two years, you would have only made 10%, or an annualized return of 5%.

If you had bought all the 1994 AFGC stocks and held them through the end of the year, your portfolio would have risen 15%.

With dividends reinvested, the S&P 500 was up a paltry 1.3% for 1994.

If you're selective, however, I think you can do even better. In each AFGC section, we profile two to four companies that we feel have the best prospects. From the beginning of 1993 to the end of 1994, this group rose more than 60%.

One of the stocks we highlighted in March 1994 was Educational Development Corporation. Don't feel bad if you've never heard of it. I hadn't either, until I noticed the company's earnings growth in our database.

Educational Development, a textbook distributor based in Tulsa, Oklahoma, is the sole distributor of books published by Usborne Publishing. The books are generally geared toward children in grades K–12, although some are advanced enough to be used as college textbooks. When we recommended it, annual sales were $8 million and total market capitalization was $11 million. Its stock was trading at $5.06.

In the fourth quarter of 1993, Educational Development's earnings rose 100%, from $0.04 to $0.08 a share. That huge earnings increase made us think we should become better educated about this company. So we did some research—and we liked what we learned.

When we examined Educational Development more closely, we were looking for signs that the earnings momentum would continue—that the great quarter wasn't a one-time event. One of the most compelling clues we found was an agreement the company had recently signed with IBM. Big Blue had decided to recommend a list of forty Usborne books as preferred reference guides through the giant computer maker's own Nature of Science software program.

The pact told us two things: (1) revenues were likely to rise smartly next year, and (2) this tiny company was distributing a high-quality product that had impressed IBM's software people. Our conversations with the company and the single analyst who followed it gave us confidence in management and in the growth outlook for the next two years.

As it turned out, both the company and the analyst underestimated how good the next year would be. (This often happens with companies experiencing torrid growth, a fact I'll address later, in the section on earnings surprises.) In the next quarter, Educational Development's earnings rose by 124%. They soared 31% in the following quarter. By December 1994, the stock hit $17.25, a gain of 241% since our recommendation just nine months before.

Did it take a genius to find out what *we* did about Educational Development? No. Was it just dumb luck? I might be tempted to say yes—except for the fact that many other companies we've spotted this way have done almost as well.

Ultimately, a stock's value hinges on just one thing: how much the company can earn per share. Or, to be more precise, how much the market *thinks* it can earn per share at some point in the future.

I have a strong bias here. I want to own stocks with the best earnings growth around—those that will turn in the most impressive comparisons next year. Yes, you can make money with a stock that increases its earnings by 10% a year, year after year, but you probably won't make a lot of money (unless you bought it for 50 cents on the dollar). I want to be better compensated for the risks I take. That's how I get maximum returns.

If you know some stock market history, you may be asking, "What about all those high fliers that crash and burn, leaving investors with stunning losses? Weren't many of them reporting huge earnings gains at one time?"

Such skepticism can be helpful—if you don't overdo it. There are very few stocks you'll want to own forever; a "widow and orphan" strategy is a bad one. I try not to overstay my welcome. I get out before the growth rate slows significantly or some bad news hits.

By the same token, total skepticism about high fliers is foolish. Research shows that fast-growing young companies often go through a cycle. Once they become profitable, they can experience extraordinary growth for five to seven years, according to Ibbotson Associates. Then the growth starts to slow substantially.

For technology companies, the high-growth phase may be compressed to three to five years—or less—but a stupendous amount of money can be made in that amount of time. Let's consider Cisco Systems, the networking hardware manufacturer. *Individual Investor* never recommended Cisco, alas, because we wrongly thought that its earnings momentum would flag sooner rather than later.

Adjusted for numerous splits, Cisco's annual earnings per share rose from just $0.02 in 1989 to $1.19 in 1994. Each year's gain was dramatic compared to the preceding year. In fact in three out of five years, the company at least doubled its earnings. In the other years, Cisco recorded earnings increases of about 86%.

During this time, Cisco's stock rose from $1.12 to $40 a share, a thirty-five-fold gain in just five years. Talk about returns!

Now, there are very few Cisco Systems around. This is one of the great stocks of all time. But it's an important case study because, at every stage of Cisco's growth, there were swarms of skeptics—myself included—who figured the company couldn't possibly do nearly as well *next* year. So they didn't buy the stock.

For most companies, the market assumes that fantastic growth is not sustainable for more than another quarter or two, if that. Find a company that can turn in terrific earnings for three, four, or five quarters, however, and you stand a great chance of realizing enormous profits.

There are many such companies out there. Like a batter on a hot streak, companies get on a roll. If a company dominates an exciting new market, it is unlikely to be dethroned overnight. And when earnings start to grow rapidly in one quarter, more quarters of oversized growth are usually on the way.

One final word about Cisco Systems. When pricing pressure finally hit the company in 1994, the stock swooned from $40 to $20 in just four months. But strong earnings gains kept coming through, and, by early 1995, the stock was back up to $37. What does this illustrate? That when high fliers disappoint their fans, the market is merciless. But once the dust settles, a company's stock price will still be determined by its earning power. Get the earnings picture right, and you can weather the inevitable declines.

FINDING THE MONEY GROWERS

The principle here may be simple, but the execution takes some work. Buying the companies with the very largest percentage gains in earnings—those that are up 100%, 200%, or more—doesn't necessarily produce optimal results.

Keep in mind that the earnings-growth numbers represent a clue, not a pat formula. Here are the criteria we use to sort through all the companies reporting 100% (or better) earnings gains for their most recent quarter.

Earnings Significance

When earnings double from a minuscule base, we're not as interested as when they grow from an already sizable foundation. Earning $0.02 per share instead of $0.01, or $0.04 rather than $0.02, tends to leave us underwhelmed. We concentrate on companies reporting earnings of at least $0.05 per share in the most recent quarter.

Revenue Growth

We prefer to see quarterly revenue gains of 25% or more. This tells us we're onto a true growth story. If, on the other hand, earnings double without significant revenue growth, the company isn't nearly as attractive. (In some cases, though, this pattern might suggest a turnaround is in progress. See Chapter 9 for more details.)

What's Going On?

Sometimes, companies report stunning earnings comparisons for the wrong reasons. What could possibly be wrong about a company that reports a 100% earnings gain? Plenty.

Maybe the company got rid of a losing division. (This could be very significant short-term but not necessarily long-term.) Or, the price of a commodity it uses in production was artificially depressed for a quarter. Or, the firm simply cut costs without increasing revenue at all. These are all fine things but are not usually the impetus for sustainable earnings growth.

Relative Value

In the previous chapter, we learned about the PEG ratio—the P/E (price/earnings) ratio for this year divided by the company's projected growth rate for next year. The PEG ratio is, in many ways, a more important indicator than the P/E ratio.

Say, for example, a fast-growing company has a P/E ratio of 40 but is expected to grow earnings by 100% next year. Dividing 100 into 40 yields 0.4, which is the PEG ratio. Anything under 1 is attractive, and anything under 0.5 is downright mouthwatering.

Expressed in simple English: I look for companies that are growing at a percentage rate significantly higher than the P/E multiple. This rule allows me to buy stocks with stratospheric P/E ratios that might scare other investors away. A company can have a P/E ratio of 80 and remain a screaming buy—if you're pretty confident that substantial earnings growth is in the cards during the next few years.

Let's say that the company with the P/E ratio of 80 is estimated to expand earnings 200% for next year, and 100% for the year after that. If those earnings projections come through, the company would have a P/E ratio of 20 two years from now, assuming the stock price doesn't change. The odds are pretty good that a company that just reported a 100% gain in annual earnings would merit a multiple higher than 20. So, if the earnings growth projection is plausible, you might want to discount that otherwise stratospheric P/E ratio.

The multiple doesn't have to stay at 80 for you to do very well. Even if the P/E ratio fell from 80 to 40, a company with these earnings would double in price in two years.

One of my rigid earnings rules is: Concentrate only on stocks whose projected three-year growth rate is higher than their P/E multiples. If a company has a P/E ratio of 15, I want it to have a projected annual growth rate of at least 20%. A 25% rate would be better. And 30% would be better still.

Let's do the math. If, right now, a $15 stock earns $1 per share today and grows at 30% for the next three years, its earnings history will look like this:

Today		$1.00
End of:	Year 1	$1.30
	Year 2	$1.69
	Year 3	$2.20

With that kind of progression, it is almost inevitable that the stock will eventually trade at a multiple that is much closer to—or perhaps even greater than—its growth rate.

If the multiple increases from 15 to 20, you'll have a $44 stock three years from now, a gain of 193%. If the multiple is 25, the stock will be $55, a gain of 267%. And if the multiple climbs to match the growth rate, the stock will be $66, a gain of 340%. Even if the multiple remains at 15, the stock will trade at $33 after three years, a rise of 120%.

Finding a stock with a low PEG ratio accomplishes two important things for me. First, it provides enormous potential if growth expectations are on target. Second, it gives me some protection if my projections are overly optimistic. If the growth rate is 20% per year instead of 25%, I should still make money.

On the other hand, when the P/E ratio is higher than the growth rate and the earnings fall slightly short of general expectations, I'll get killed. And I'll regret ever having heard of this stock that was growing fast—but not nearly fast enough to justify its lofty multiple.

Profit Margins

When a fast-growing company is really healthy, its profit margin— the percentage of revenues that ultimately end up as earnings— should be expanding. In classic investment theory, companies with wider profit margins are worth more than those with thin margins, because the high-margin companies will be able to earn more money faster than the low-margin companies. Given this truism, it stands to reason that companies with expanding profit margins are more attractive than those with receding margins, or less profitability.

Expanding margins were one of the signals that brought us to Educational Development. In 1992, its net profit margin was 9%. In the third quarter of 1993, the margin jumped to 14%.

If you find a company with strong and growing profit margins, the odds are good that it is in an attractive business and that its management knows what to do. Rising profit margins are an important sign of management competence.

Market Position

With relatively few exceptions, I like to buy companies that dominate a market or a particular niche. For such companies, rapid earnings growth is more likely to be sustainable.

This is only logical. Companies with dominant positions have more pricing flexibility and are less likely to be the victims of predatory pricing by a competitor. Furthermore, if the niche is narrow enough, these companies can grow like gangbusters for years without attracting competition from a corporate giant intent on invading their turf. (If the market gets big enough, though, the giants may start to attack.)

THE RECURRENCE FACTOR

When should you buy? How many quarters of great earnings are enough? When should too many good quarters scare you away? The answers to these questions depend on your individual personality, but some general rules can be applied.

In many cases, one blowout quarter may be sufficient for you to take the investment plunge, if your research indicates that the next few years look very strong. If you want to be more conservative, however, don't buy until a company reports its second consecutive quarter of triple-digit growth. That's a more powerful signal.

When should you be afraid that there has already been too much good news? I'll discuss this more thoroughly in Chapter 9, "When to Sell," but here are some signs that the story may already have become a little stale:

- New competitors are entering the company's market.

- After four, six, or eight quarters of incredible growth, the company's P/E multiple is so high that it seems as if the market is expecting this growth to last forever. (And you're skeptical enough to know that it won't.)

- Profit margins have stopped growing or have begun to shrink.

- The company's relative strength is 99. Relative strength—reported each day in *Investor's Business Daily*—is expressed as a percentile. A ranking of 99 means that a stock has outperformed 99% of all other stocks over the past six months. This is the highest relative-strength ranking a stock can have, and it means that a lot of the good news has already been factored in.

   I don't automatically avoid stocks with a relative strength ranking of 99, but it does give me pause. I'd prefer to see a relative strength of 85, 90, or 95, rather than 99. Again, I think this adds to my margin of safety.

EARNINGS SURPRISES

Happiness is a positive earnings surprise in a stock you own. Several wonderful things happen when a company's earnings exceed the consensus forecast of analysts who follow the company.

Analysts revise their earnings forecasts upward, and new buyers flock to the stock. Best of all, money managers who specialize in stocks that surprise analysts begin taking positions in the company.

Generally speaking, unless the company suggests that rougher days lie ahead, you shouldn't sell a stock right after a positive surprise. Small stocks can spike up dramatically after such news.

There's another reason not to sell: Companies that surprise on the upside often do so more than once. A company that exceeds expectations has momentum behind it, and positive momentum—as we've seen—often continues for many quarters. Analysts estimate earnings largely from information gathered from the company. Some companies chronically disappoint investors because management is always promising that prosperity is just around the corner—and it never is. Other companies frequently serve up pleasant surprises because management is conservative in its projections, and because earnings are growing so fast that it's hard to tell precisely how high they'll be three months from now.

Earlier, I mentioned MicroTouch, the nation's leading producer of touch screens for computers and ATMs. In August 1994, the company reported earnings of $0.37 per share on revenues of $141.1 million. Earnings were up 164% and were 50% higher than the consensus estimate of $0.25 per share. It was an incredible quarter. Not surprisingly, the stock rose that week to $15, a three-point increase.

Our *Special Situations Report* had recently re-recommended the stock at $5.50, so we were happy—but that didn't mean we knew what to do next. Some people on my staff wanted us to sell and take profits. I had a different view.

After speaking with the analysts who follow the company, I determined that this was a classic earnings surprise situation. What does that mean? The people who had followed the company most closely knew that earnings would be terrific again next quarter, but no one was confident about the number that could be put on that projection.

In cases like this, uncertainty is a negative, but when a company is on a roll, uncertainty can work in your favor. Because it is hard for analysts to predict monster earnings, their tendency is to be conservative. When their hesitation proves unfounded, the company reports better-than-expected earnings numbers and investors respond by pushing the stock higher.

MicroTouch reported another surprisingly wonderful quarter in September. Earnings were well above the consensus estimate. After that knockout quarter, we sold our position at $30—double the price we would have received three months earlier.

And we still left some money on the table. MicroTouch hit $47.50 a month after we sold it. After that, it began falling back to more reasonable levels.

EARNINGS WATCH

In every issue of *Individual Investor*, there's a page called Earnings Watch. The four tables on the page can be very valuable in different ways.

The first two list the 25 companies with the greatest increase and decrease in consensus earnings estimates for the coming year, as tabulated by I/B/E/S, a New York City firm that tracks analysts' projections for every publicly traded company.

Smart investors realize that whenever earnings estimates are being adjusted, it's unlikely that the consensus will be right the first time. Usually, the trend goes further than people expect.

Companies whose earnings estimates are being adjusted upward deserve a special look. They'll be more likely than an average company to surprise on the upside next quarter or next year. Companies whose earnings are being adjusted downward should be avoided like the plague.

FEAR OF TORRID GROWTH

I want to say a bit more about why some smart people wrongly avoid stocks with blockbuster earnings. These investors don't want to be suckers. Conservative investors and value investors, in particular, just naturally shy away from any stock with a high P/E ratio. And stocks with fast-growing earnings almost always have high P/E ratios.

Instead of automatically looking the other way, I wish these investors would ask: "Why is this company achieving such extraordinary earnings at this particular time? Does it have a new hit product? New management? Are the margins showing dramatic improvement? Will it profit from new legislation? Is it in the right place to capitalize on a powerful new trend?"

WHY GO AFTER BIG GAME?

People often ask why my earnings screening methodology is so arbitrary. Aren't there great companies out there growing by less than 100% per quarter?

Yes. In my own research, I'll investigate all companies reporting earnings gains of 50%. But that's my cutoff for the earnings screen. I may invest in a company growing at 33% because I see heavy insider buying, but I'll discover it because of the insider transactions, not because of the earnings gains.

I think it's important to be rigid. My time, like yours, is limited. (Yours is presumably more limited. Looking for fast-growing companies is my day job.) The stock market is always about opportunity cost. At any moment, you want your money to be in the best stocks possible. You should have a strong reason for believing that a stock you buy will do better than every other possible investment. Extraordinary earnings growth can help guide you to this type of winner.

Concentrating on the biggest earnings gainers also works because it helps you stay selective. Selectivity is a key to long-term profits. You never *have* to make a trade. You don't need to find a new idea every day. My goal is to find 10 to 20 great stocks a year. Warren Buffett, arguably the greatest investor in American history, says he tries to find a single great idea a year. Just one.

When you're thinking of buying a new stock, you should never feel pressured by time. This isn't some football game in which you have to play catch-up to win. There's no clock ticking away as you read this book.

A "Conservative" Approach to Great Earnings

One great place to start looking for earnings growth is in the specialty retail sector. Retail stocks may offer a fairly conservative way to invest for maximum returns. They are easy to track, for one thing. Every month, retailers report same-store sales growth. It's a simple concept.

Let's look at one of my biggest winners, Michaels Stores. Michaels, based in Irving, Texas, is the nation's leading retailer of arts and crafts supplies. The company was reporting 18% to 22% same-store sales growth in 1991 when I recommended it, and it kept racking up double-digit increases for years. At the time of my initial recommendation, Michaels was selling at a P/E ratio of just 14, which, given its sales trend, was ridiculously cheap.

With competent management, such same-store sales increases almost invariably translate into runaway earnings gains. That's what happened with Michaels.

To make the earnings picture even rosier, Michaels added new stores quickly and, in 1994, bought out its largest competitor. Result: Earnings have risen at an annual rate of 83% since 1990. During that time, Michaels stock rose nine fold—well over 300% since our recommendation.

Retailers also disclose their expansion strategy regularly and clearly. They will tell you how many stores they plan to open next year and where many of those stores will be. Note that the same-store sales numbers are far more important than overall sales gains. In fact, a retailer whose store base and aggregate revenues are expanding rapidly at the same time that same-store sales are declining is probably heading for big trouble.

How to Proceed

When you find an earnings story that intrigues you, here's what to do.

- Call the company to get more information. Ask the investor relations department to mail or fax you the press release that accompanies the earnings. How can a press release have credibility and value? Because it is a public document released by a regulated company. Lawyers have gone over it very carefully. If it's misleading, the company will be sued by disgruntled shareholders.

  If, therefore, the release tells you that the coming quarters look strong, they probably will be. (Just don't expect a money-back guarantee.) Or, if the release discloses that earnings are unlikely to show big gains next year, that's your signal to look elsewhere.

- If you're still interested, have the company send you its financials (annual report, recent quarterly reports, forms 10-K and 10-Q, and proxy statements). You want to learn as much as possible about this company before you buy it.

- Ask the company's investor relations person to give you the names and phone numbers of analysts who follow the stock (this list can be included in the initial package). Then call to get their latest research reports.

  You're allowed to do this. If the reports are bullish, the analysts will be happy to send them along. They want to find buyers for the stocks they like (at least partly because buying pressure will make them look like better analysts).

- After digesting the reports, you can call the analyst or the company's head of investor relations to ask questions. Don't just listen to the words you hear. Pay attention to the tone as well. Are these people candid or promotional? Does the story sound like the ultimate in blue-sky hype, or does it strike you as a reasonable strategy that a decently managed company should be able to execute? Form your own opinion. Don't be swayed by market expectations.

I talk to and meet with corporate managers all the time. What do I look for in these meetings? Certainly not wild-eyed optimism. I want someone who outlines a sober business strategy without any hype.

If several companies appeal to you but you can buy only one right now, compare their growth rates, multiples, and balance sheets. See where the stocks are trading today compared to a week ago, a month ago, and a year ago. Check their relative strength ranking in *Investor's Business Daily*. Your goal is to find the stock that is better than all the others you might buy today.

Now That You're an Owner

Whenever you own a stock, it's important that you have specific earnings expectations for the coming quarter and the coming year.

If you think XYZ will earn 20 cents a share next quarter and, instead, it merely breaks even, you might want to unload the stock immediately and cut your losses. Something is amiss.

At the very least, call the company and ask some tough questions. Why are inventories so high? Why is sales growth slowing? Why are profit margins under pressure? Only some very good answers should convince you to hold on.

In any case, take notes on these conversations and save them in the file you keep on the company. You'll want to test management's answers against future results. Do the company's answers bear any relation to reality or are they just wishful thinking?

If XYZ does earn 20 cents and the stock heads down anyway, you should reassess your position. Do more research. Get the company's press release. Talk to the company and to analysts. Has the stock's outlook worsened even though this quarter's earnings came through as expected?

Often, a downturn is just the result of normal stock market unpredictability. If you like the company's story every bit as much as you did before, think of using the price decline to add to your position. After all, the company itself is doing what you expected it to do. If it keeps beating expectations, other investors will eventually climb aboard.

If the results exceed your expectations, you might also want to increase your holdings, but don't forget to start thinking about your exit strategy. At a certain point, when good news about a company is simply too obvious to ignore, the stock price may be propelled to a level that will be unsustainable.

Should you set a price objective when you buy a stock? If you're truly seeking maximum returns, the answer is no. I never set price targets. Instead, I often sell off a portion of my holdings if a stock doubles.

After a stock you own has made a big upward move, calmly reassess the fundamentals. I always compare the P/E ratio on the company's last twelve months of earnings (LTM) with its projected growth rate. I want to know if I'm still getting good value. If the earnings come through as expected, do I think the stock will rise significantly? If the answer is yes and there are no other apparent problems, I hold on.

EARNINGS STORIES TO AVOID

I always try to go beyond the earnings numbers—and sometimes my attempt costs me money.

I intentionally avoided two of the hottest stocks of the 1990s—Snapple Beverage and Starbucks—despite their run of extraordinary earnings gains. What turned me off?

It wasn't the quality of the products, which was high in both cases. Nor did I think either was benefiting from a fad that was sure to fade. I was troubled by the companies' high profit margins in businesses that had negligible barriers to entry (a coffee bar is not that difficult to open). Eventually, frenzied competition in both niches was absolutely predictable. The erosion of margins had to happen.

Furthermore, I'm always wary of companies in which short sellers have been so active. When a stock is this controversial, it often ends up crashing—maybe later rather than sooner. But later can seem pretty soon if you're still in the stock. Snapple was 60% off its 1993 high when Quaker Oats acquired it at $13 in 1994. And, as we went to press, Starbucks was down 25% from its best level.

TURNAROUNDS

I'm always looking for companies that report their first quarter of positive earnings in a while. If the company is a large-cap stock and the earnings were completely expected, that's not very exciting. But, for small, underfollowed stocks, an earnings turnaround can represent a great opportunity.

Why? Because, very often, the reversal of fortune is unexpected. It also frequently goes unnoticed—at least at first.

Generally, when once-profitable companies start spurting red ink, their stocks get crushed, killed, and buried. People naturally start thinking of worst-case scenarios. Maybe the company's time has passed. Perhaps it will never earn money again. Someday, it might even totter into bankruptcy.

When bad news flows for more than a quarter or two, some predictable things happen on Wall Street. Professional analysts are only allowed to be wrongly bullish for so long. So the analysts who were once bullish on the company slash their estimates and their ratings. Then they're expected to capitulate. Soon, the only person on the Street with a buy rating is an analyst who works for the underwriter who brought the company public—and nobody believes the underwriter anymore.

Eventually, maybe even he or she changes the tune. The stock becomes a true orphan, an issue that is unloved and unfollowed. Almost every professional will ignore this kind of stock. On Wall Street, people get paid for avoiding this kind of stock, for pretending it hardly exists. The only people who care about it passionately will probably hate it—because it has been such a disappointment.

And because they, poor souls, may still own it.

Sometimes, though, earnings happily turn around. One striking example is Caere Corp., an information recognition software company. In 1993 Caere got as high as $26, but then it stopped making money. By the second quarter of 1994 it had fallen all the way to $6.

I noticed Caere when it reported its earnings in July 1994. The stock was then at $8. It earned six cents a share for the quarter. That's hardly impressive if you annualize the earnings—four times six is 24 and that would give you an above-market P/E of 33—but when a company is turning around you don't annualize the earnings this way. You start to wonder what it could earn if things that were going wrong started going right.

Had people been getting goofy when they bid Caere's price up to $26 a year earlier, or was that an entirely reasonable valuation for a company with its potential? There was only one way to find out.

We went through our usual steps: contacting the company for press releases and financials, talking to the managers, talking to analysts, looking for insider transactions, etc.

Interestingly, Caere stock didn't budge immediately on the good earnings announcement. The movement came a bit later. This is typical for a beaten-down company with no institutional backing. Once you've disappointed investors, you're not easily forgiven. After all, who wants to get burned by the same stock twice? How do you explain that to your clients or your spouse? This environment of doubt creates a terrific opportunity for the individual investor. It gives you time to analyze the company carefully after the first piece of good news. Odds are, the stock won't run away from you.

Here's what happened with Caere. As the next quarter's earnings approached, the stock gradually worked its way higher. It was sitting at $10 just before the earnings were announced, which meant a gain of 27% in three months. But the real fun hadn't started.

On October 1994, Caere announced earnings of $0.15 a share for the quarter, compared with a loss of $0.15 the previous year. Within a week, the stock shot up five points on enormous volume, a gain of 49%. Now it was up 88% in three months.

Caere's potential was there for all to see. It just took a little work.

4

What Do They Know?

INVESTING WITH THE INSIDERS

Between 1990 and 1993, a company called Ampex posted more than $31 per share in losses. Ampex—a decades-old company that is attributed with inventing the technology behind the videocassette recorder—once boasted a market capitalization larger than that of Xerox. As it began 1995, however, Ampex had a shareholders' deficit of $195 million, and looked like the epitome of a company on its last legs.

When *Individual Investor* discovered Ampex in April 1995, its stock was trading for $1.75 per share on the lowly OTC Bulletin Board. Normally, we would ignore such an issue. But one fact led us to take a look at Ampex: Edward Bramson, chairman of the company, had recently purchased 1.5 million shares for an average price of $1.61 each—a $2.4 million investment.

Was Ampex ripe for a turnaround? Bramson certainly seemed confident enough to place such a large bet on his company's future. What's more, Bramson already owned 4.5 million shares of Ampex before his latest purchase. He already had a lot riding on Ampex's future, and yet he chose to up his ownership stake to 17%.

As we expected, Bramson knew that things were going well for his firm. Profit margins improved throughout 1995 as the company continued to shed non-core businesses and focus on a new line of digital storage products, and royalty income on older products also remained healthy. Ampex's shareholders' deficit was reduced by one-third during the year, and its stock moved up to the American Stock Exchange early in 1996.

The stock price also moved up. It ended 1995 at $4. But we felt it could go higher because of the promise of a new technology developed by the company to increase the speed and capacity of computer hard drives. This "keepering" technology resulted from one of the thousands of patents Ampex owns, and is presently being assessed for commercial viability by several manufacturers.

Apparently, the market agreed with our assessment of the potential of keepering. By the summer of 1996, Ampex's shares were trading for more than $7, about four times greater than what insider Bramson had paid for them many months earlier.

For all investors, myself included, it's impossible to know what the insiders know. But you can know what they *do*. Often, that's enough of a signal. In fact, insider buying is my single favorite stock-picking indicator. It is a great place to start when you're looking for big winners.

(Insiders have such a tremendous investment advantage that in the 1930s—when the Securities and Exchange Commission (SEC) was established—there were discussions about banning all insider trading activity. The regulators worried that it was simply too easy for insiders to buy low and sell high.)

Part of what I love about insider buying information is that it is a black-and-white indicator. Insiders open their wallets to buy their stock for only one reason—the same reason that drives you and me: They want to make money.

Unlike the rest of us, however, insiders have an enormous edge. They know more about their companies than we can ever hope to learn. As an investor, I found this out many years ago. More recently, I've gained even more insight into the process in my role as the chairman and CEO of a public company, Individual Investor Group.

I can't predict exactly what's going to happen to my business next year, but it's fairly easy to tell when the trend is up and when it is down—and *why*. In my company's case, I'll have circulation figures for *Individual Investor* magazine in my hands long before any outsider sees them, and I'm among the first to know how ad sales are running. I'm also privy to the performance figures of our money-management subsidiary, and I know when we are about to proceed with an important acquisition. You can see how early access to this kind of information would be a tremendous advantage for me as an investor in my own company.

It's hardly surprising, then, that study after study shows that when insiders buy, their track record is phenomenal. When insiders bet their own money on a company's prospects, they're giving you the best tip you can possibly get.

It makes perfect sense that, of all the stocks in the world, insiders choose to invest in the stock of the company where they work. Given the fact that the insiders already have a sizable financial stake in the business—salary, bonus, stock, options—isn't it interesting that they have picked this moment not to diversify but to increase their financial dependence on the fortunes of their company? That speaks volumes to me.

A DEFINITION

Before we go any further, let's be absolutely clear about our definition of insider buying. I'm referring to the legal variety—the transactions that insiders must register with the SEC by the tenth day of the month after their trade occurs. The SEC definition of an insider includes all officers and directors, as well as any individual who owns 10% or more of a company's stock.

That reporting requirement—which, unfortunately, isn't always honored in a timely manner by all insiders—actually helps individual investors. They can see exactly what the insiders are doing.

Certain SEC restrictions on insiders help the individual investor as well. For instance, insiders cannot actively trade their own stocks. Once they buy, they must hold their purchase for at least 60 days. So, when you learn that an insider has bought 50,000 shares, it's almost always true that he or she still owns those recently purchased shares.

Insiders are also prohibited from profiting from relevant non-public information. In this category is any news the general public doesn't have—news that would cause the stock to move if the information were widely known. For example, insiders can't buy right before the announcement of great earnings, or a big new contract, or a takeover. That delay is intended to help level the information playing field for outsiders.

AN EARLY CLUE

Knowing about insider buying can boost your returns in two ways:

1. It helps align you with some of the savviest investors on Wall Street.
2. It allows you to discover hidden gems early.

By tracking insider transactions, you have a wonderful source for new ideas about little-known companies. You can zero in on great profit-making opportunities before most other investors discover them.

For the majority of publicly traded companies, insider transaction information may be the only source of opinion available. No analysts followed Ampex, for example. And no analysts followed Kendall International when we recommended it in May 1993.

At the time, Kendall, which makes wound-care products (including Curad bandages) had $775 million in annual revenues. But it wasn't profitable, and it was still trying to work out from under more than $1 billion in debt (some of it at junk-bond interest rates of 15%) that it had taken on in a nearly disastrous 1988 leveraged buyout. Like Prins's balance sheet, Kendall's wasn't a pretty sight.

Kendall went public in 1992. A year later, a group of insiders began buying heavily at an average price of $25.80. Among them was chief financial officer (CFO) Alexander Castaldi, who invested $200,000. That amount is a bell-ringer. Why? Because the CFO isn't nearly as well compensated as the chairman or president. For most CFOs, Castaldi included, $200,000 is a huge commitment. Many of them don't earn that in a year. Castaldi was investing a huge portion of his annual income in one stock. Most of us have never done that. It was an enormous show of confidence from someone who should have had a pretty good sense of whether the company's sorry balance sheet would soon look better—or worse.

And Castaldi was by no means alone. Kendall's president was also a buyer, as were the controller and a director. Together, the three of them paid almost $90,000 for additional Kendall shares.

After the flurry of insider buying, business began improving at Kendall. Sales grew smartly, and cost-cutting improved the earnings picture. The company took advantage of lower interest rates to refinance some of its burdensome debt.

Nine months after we wrote about Kendall, the stock had doubled. After a year, it was up 148%. Shortly after that, Tyco Labs acquired Kendall for $63.88 per share.

Getting the Information

Insider transaction information is not privileged, although in some forms it can be expensive. Here's a list of resources that provide that information. (Even if you decide not to track insider transactions directly, I think it's important that you pay close attention to such information when you see it mentioned in articles or analysts' reports.)

- The best online source for insider transactions is the Washington Service, which I use in my office. As soon as an insider reports a transaction to the SEC, it shows up on my screen. There's no time lag.

- The most comprehensive print source is the *Insiders' Chronicle* ($445 per year), a weekly newsletter that reports every single trade insiders make.

- Every week, both *Barron's* and *The Wall Street Journal* have short features on insider transactions. I find them fairly superficial, but they do have one great advantage. If you already get the publications, they're absolutely free.

- I am such a believer in its value that I include two pages of articles and two pages of data on insider transaction information in every issue of *Individual Investor*. Our "Insider's Edge" section attempts to take you behind the scenes at four or five companies where there has been hefty recent insider buying.

WHAT TO LOOK FOR

Insider buying is always a good sign, but the following factors can make it an even more powerful indicator.

Transaction Size

You learn that an insider has been putting personal money into his or her company, but you want to know how much money. More is better, although you cannot measure this maxim in pure dollar terms. Always take into account the market capitalization of the company and the number of outstanding shares.

Tiny Cypros Pharmaceuticals is a perfect example. At the end of June 1993, Bernard Levine, a company director, bought 100,000 shares of the development-stage drug company at $4.50. Any $450,000 investment is nothing to sneeze at, but what made this one jump out at us was the huge percentage of total shares that Levine's purchase represented.

At the time, Cypros had only 2.4 million shares, so Levine was snapping up 4% of the company in a single open-market transaction. Insiders rarely buy so much of a company all at once. Even more dramatic was the fact that Cypros had a float of only 1.1 million shares. Levine was buying 9% of the available shares.

We highlighted Cypros in September 1993 at $4.75. By early January 1994, the stock had hit $12.50, a remarkable jump of 163%. What had happened? The company received FDA (Food and Drug Administration) approval to market two drugs designed to dissolve blood clots associated with heart attacks and strokes. Levine made a big bet in advance that this would happen.

What Do They Know?

Strategies

Guide to *Insider* Transactions

FORM 4s: INSIDER BUYING

Company	Ticker Symbol	Transaction Value	# of Shares Purchased	# of Insiders- Rel. to Co.¹	Trade Date(s)	Average Transact. Price	Recent Price	52-Week High	52-Week Low	Latest 12 Month EPS	PE	Shares Out. (mil.)	Telephone #
Enron Global Power/Pipln.	EPP	76,025,756	2,930,831	2 - S,B	6/18	25.94	23.63	27.00	21.00	1.71	13.8	20.9	(713) 853-1937
Cellular Communications	COMMA	60,429,481	1,134,757	3 - B,B,B	5/17-6/28	53.25	52.88	55.00	45.25	1.31	40.4	13.0	(212) 906-8440
Financial Sec. Assurance	FSA	53,000,000	2,000,000	2 - D,B	6/17	26.50	26.63	28.38	24.00	2.34	11.4	31.3	(212) 826-0100
Rhone-Poulenc Rorer	RPR	46,063,660	771,000	1 - B	5/6-6/17	59.75	66.63	69.25	40.38	2.40	27.8	135.6	(610) 454-8000
Conseco, Incorporated	CNC	36,358,735	932,335	8 - D,D,F,O,C,O,D	5/20-5/24	39.00	38.50	40.75	23.38	5.03	7.7	41.8	(317) 817-6100
Fifth Third Bancorp	FITB	30,469,982	561,976	1 - B	5/8-6/26	54.22	50.50	59.50	36.33	3.01	16.8	102.3	(513) 579-5300
DMX	TUNE	20,400,000	10,200,000	1 - B	5/13-5/14	2.00	1.06	3.31	0.81	-0.66	N/A	43.6	(310) 444-1744
Delta Air Lines	DAL	13,640,910	167,800	1 - D	5/7-6/18	81.39	79.50	87.00	63.50	3.11	25.6	51.4	(404) 715-2600
RFS Hotel Investors	RFSI	12,736,745	760,500	4 - D,P,F,P	5/21-6/21	16.75	15.63	18.50	13.75	1.29	12.1	24.3	(901) 767-5154
Mycogen Corporation	MYCO	12,350,700	687,500	3 - B,B,B	5/2-6/14	17.96	14.75	20.00	7.75	-1.79	N/A	30.6	(619) 453-8030
Human Genome Sciences	HGSI	10,885,182	271,248	2 - B,B	6/10	40.13	35.63	49.75	18.25	-1.33	N/A	18.7	(301) 309-8504
Marvel Entertainment	MRV	10,000,000	1,000,000	1 - C	6/25	10.00	9.63	16.50	9.38	-0.61	N/A	101.8	(212) 696-0808
Gartner Group	GART	9,181,250	267,500	1 - B	6/24-6/27	34.32	36.00	43.13	13.13	0.37	97.3	90.8	(203) 964-0096
National Insurance Group	NAIG	8,655,098	824,295	1 - D	5/23	10.50	5.88	7.50	4.25	-0.96	N/A	4.7	(415) 872-6772
Extended Stay America	STAY	6,665,000	215,000	1 - D	5/31	31.00	30.75	35.00	20.00	-0.10	N/A	32.6	(954) 713-1600
ERC Industries	ERCI	5,981,539	7,384,616	1 - B	6/6	0.81	0.94	1.13	0.66	-0.06	N/A	13.9	(713) 398-8901
Freeport McMoRan	FTX	5,465,462	150,000	1 - D	5/1-5/13	36.44	37.50	44.50	20.15	15.42	2.4	27.1	(504) 582-4000
AES	AESC	4,800,000	200,000	1 - P	5/28	24.00	30.50	31.13	18.50	1.46	20.9	75.0	(703) 522-1315
Interpublic Group	IPG	4,196,700	90,000	1 - C	5/30	46.63	46.50	50.25	35.50	1.69	27.5	79.2	(212) 399-8000
American Financial Group	AFG	4,080,553	133,821	2 - D,O	5/8-6/10	30.49	30.13	34.50	25.25	4.18	7.2	60.9	(513) 579-2121
Allied Waste Industries	AWIN	4,002,464	492,308	2 - C,P	6/21	8.13	9.00	10.38	6.38	3.18	50.0	50.8	(602) 423-2946
WMX Technologies	WMX	3,317,388	101,100	3 - D,O,P	6/11-6/27	32.81	32.13	36.13	26.38	1.41	22.8	496.1	(708) 572-8800
Orthodontic Centers of Am	OCAI	2,940,900	100,000	1 - C	6/21-6/24	29.41	31.25	41.50	12.00	0.49	63.8	21.1	(904) 273-0004
Pennī DataComm Networks	PNRL	2,769,170	205,000	4 - S,S,S,S	6/19-6/28	13.51	13.13	14.13	4.38	-1.41	N/A	10.5	(301) 417-0552
Smart & Final	SMF	2,461,148	100,455	2 - B,D	6/3	24.50	25.38	26.00	16.38	0.91	27.9	20.3	(213) 589-1054
First Industrial Realty	FR	2,440,038	103,000	1 - S	6/3-6/28	23.69	23.00	25.00	19.38	0.62	37.1	24.1	(312) 704-9000
Drew Industries	DW	2,407,450	171,850	8 - D,D,O,D,U,D,F	5/24-6/28	14.01	17.13	18.50	11.38	1.67	10.3	5.5	(914) 428-9098
Willamette Industries	WMTT	2,205,169	36,878	1 - T	5/31-6/19	59.80	58.00	72.75	48.75	8.86	6.5	55.2	(503) 227-5581
Aerosonic Corporation	AIM	2,174,000	1,087,000	1 - C	5/23	2.00	2.69	3.13	1.25	-0.31	N/A	3.8	(813) 461-3000
Modine Manufacturing	MODI	2,020,177	80,007	1 - S	6/19	25.25	25.50	40.50	22.50	2.02	12.6	29.7	(414) 636-1200
Seaman Furniture Company	SEAM	1,939,230	104,500	2 - D,D	5/7-6/13	18.56	17.56	21.00	15.00	0.78	22.5	4.5	(516) 496-9560
Shelby Williams Ind.	SY	1,882,750	179,000	2 - C,C	6/25-6/28	10.52	11.13	13.50	10.13	0.81	13.7	9.8	(312) 527-3593
Travelers Group	TRV	1,796,325	46,350	2 - D,O	5/3-5/6	38.75	44.50	47.25	29.39	4.03	11.0	476.4	(212) 816-8000
Transatlantic Holdings	TRH	1,692,490	27,000	1 - B	5/8-5/9	62.68	68.50	75.25	62.38	6.00	11.4	23.0	(212) 770-2000
Lone Star Technologies	LSST	1,649,270	182,400	2 - B,C	5/6-6/12	9.04	12.13	12.88	7.50	0.52	23.3	20.5	(214) 386-3981
Plains Resources	PLX	1,568,616	143,629	3 - B,B,D	5/7-6/7	10.92	12.13	13.00	6.75	0.92	13.2	15.3	(713) 654-1414
Daniel Green Company	DAGR	1,501,000	475,000	1 - C	6/26	3.16	3.25	5.50	2.50	-1.01	N/A	1.0	(315) 429-3131
American Classic Voyages	AMCV	1,495,400	200,000	2 - B,D	6/24-6/28	7.48	7.38	13.25	7.00	-3.55	N/A	13.8	(312) 258-1890
E'Town Corporation	ETW	1,495,000	52,000	3 - D,O,O	6/7	28.75	28.13	30.50	25.50	2.13	13.2	7.6	(908) 654-1234
Northrop Grumman	NOC	1,265,000	20,000	1 - D	6/3	63.25	67.38	69.25	52.63	5.24	12.9	57.7	(310) 553-6262
DeKalb Genetics	SEEDB	1,194,187	47,300	1 - B	6/25-6/28	25.25	27.25	30.50	12.92	0.87	31.3	13.4	(815) 758-3461

KEY Definitions. An **insider** is an officer or director of a company, or an individual or entity owning 10% or more of a company's stock. A **Form 4** is the SEC document filed by insiders who buy or sell their company's stock. The transaction must be registered by the tenth day of the month after the trade occurs. A **Form 144** is the SEC document filed by holders of restricted securities to provide notice of intent to sell. ¹Insider Relation codes: A-affiliated person; B-Beneficial owner of more than 10% of the company's shares; C-chairman of the board; D-director; F-chief financial officer of treasurer; G-general partner; L-limited partner; O-officer; P-president or chief executive officer; S-shareholder; T-trustee; U-unknown; V-vice president.

Lists are ranked by transaction value of filings registered with the Securities and Exchange Commission (SEC) during the four weeks ended July 12, 1996.
Source: Form 4 and 144 data provided by Washington Service Associates, Washington, D.C.

INDIVIDUAL INVESTOR, SEPTEMBER 1996

Number of Buyers

I like to see cluster buying. If three or four insiders have decided that their stock is undervalued, I'm impressed. My odds of being right are improved, and I like any bit of information that makes my job easier.

In some cases, though, cluster buying may not mean what it seems to mean. Generally, I don't like to see four executives buy their stock on the same day. That smacks of a coordinated effort and makes me nervous. I prefer to see cluster buying over a period of weeks or months.

Occasionally, group buying news really *is* too good to be true. If you saw that eleven insiders had bought 2,152 shares apiece at a publicly traded bank, you might think of buying as well, right? Don't; this probably isn't real buying. Banks often give out shares as part of employee compensation. The employees who are getting the shares have to fill out the standard SEC insider transaction forms.

The Caliber of the Buyers

I want to see the people who know the most about the entire company do the buying. Who's best informed? I would rank potential buyers in descending order as follows:

- Active chairman of the board.
- Chief executive officer.
- Inactive chairman of the board (not involved in day-to-day operations).
- Chief operating officer.
- Chief financial officer.
- Company directors.
- Other company executives.

Occasionally, many top people in a company will start buying—and that's a beautiful thing. It's what happened with CACI International.

When we wrote about CACI International in January 1994, the stock was at $6 and the company was in transition. For years, it had sold its software to the Defense Department, but now that business was fading. CACI was trying to turn itself into a technology company focusing on business.

Lots of companies decide to follow what's hot and abandon what's not. It's an old story. Sometimes it works, and sometimes it is an investment horror show, complete with perennial promises that "Next year, we'll finally get it right. Trust us." Almost every veteran investor has been burned by one of these stories.

But CACI was succeeding. The company won 15 of the 17 business contracts it bid on in 1993, and increased its backlog by 70%. Wall Street took some notice, but not much. For me, however, the insider buying by a group of key personnel suggested that CACI's transformation was real and not just wishful thinking.

Alan Parsow, owner of 12% of CACI's stock, had several of his investment vehicles buy more than 80,000 shares at prices ranging from $4.06 to $4.56. The company's chairman, president, and CFO all bought as well. Their purchases weren't large, but the unanimity of opinion was definitely encouraging.

CACI continued to win contracts and penetrate the business market. By late April 1994, the stock had hit $10.38, a 73% gain from the time we spotted it, and a stunning 156% jump from the low price paid by insiders.

Relative Size of the Purchase

More shares are usually better, but not always. I like to see an individual make a purchase that represents a significant outlay *for that person*. If a billionaire chairman buys an additional 10,000 shares of a $5 stock, that's nice—but it doesn't make me want to rush out and buy. (If the chairman is wrong, he'll live. If you follow his incorrect lead, the loss may be quite unpleasant for you.)

When a vice president who earns $150,000 a year buys $25,000 worth of his company's shares, that's a big commitment. It is a real sign that something good may be happening at the company.

Percentage of Holdings the Purchase Represents

Ideally, you want to find insiders who are dramatically increasing their stake in a company. Ask: What percentage of the individual's total holdings are accounted for by these new purchases?

One of the reasons we were attracted to American Medical Holdings was that president John Casey bought 20,000 shares at $10.50 in July 1993. It wasn't the $210,000 transaction size that was so exciting. It was the fact that Casey had tripled his stake in the company.

Most purchases by company presidents are more incremental. Casey's buy was a whopper—and as pure a forecast for an earnings surge as we could have found. It was correct, too. Profits soon soared, and dragged the stock along. American Medical Holdings was at $13.25 when we featured it. By the end of the year, it had doubled in price.

All things being equal, it's far better to find a situation where insiders are doubling or tripling their stakes rather than adding an incremental 1% or 2%. New buying by an insider who owns no shares may also be a terrific signal—with one important exception. When new directors join a company's board, they often make token purchases of the stock. In many cases, the significance of this buying is more social and political than it is financial. Ignore it.

Track Record of Buyers

Some investors are better than others. I believe in following the actions of insiders and the actions of great investors. But some great investors are also insiders. Their actions deserve special attention.

I also care how well a buyer—whether a legendary investor or not—has done with his or her previous insider purchases. Some executives, after all, have been known to misjudge their company's strength at any particular moment. Others seem to have a knack for assessing their company's fortunes accurately. When they buy, their stock is a bargain; when they sell (if they sell), it is temporarily overpriced.

One of the reasons we made the nation's leading industrial foam producer, Foamex International, a Magic 25 choice for 1995 was that chairman Marshall Cogan had purchased 200,000 shares for about $2 million. Cogan is a very rich man who already owned 42% of Foamex, which has a market capitalization of $200 million. So why did we care about his $2 million purchase?

Because $2 million is a major outlay for anyone, with the possible exception of Bill Gates. Successful people don't throw around seven-figure sums without careful thought.

Then there is Cogan's history. He has consistently proved to be a savvy insider, buying low and selling high. We thought history just might repeat itself and, of course, we liked Foamex's business prospects as well.

It won't be easy for you to get this kind of information on your own, but pay special attention if you see it mentioned in an article.

Industry Patterns

From time to time, insider buying sweeps through an industry. This is extremely bullish.

It means that competing companies think the prospects for the sector are improving. Finding such a consensus improves your odds. Would you rather buy into a sector that is emerging from a trough or one that is about to fall off a cliff?

In the middle of 1992, executives at leading computer chip companies (Intel, Texas Instruments, Motorola, and Micron Technology) began a wave of insider buying. At that time semiconductor stocks were the best performing group in the entire market. During that period, Intel, Texas Instruments, Motorola, and Micron Technology were universally beloved by Wall Street analysts and the investors who follow their advice.

Some stocks did better than others, and people who selected Micron were happier than those who bought the other companies. (*Individual Investor* happened to recommend Micron at $8, and it then rose about 300% in 18 months. We, and our readers, were very happy.) But even the worst performer of the four chip-makers rose far more than the overall market did during that period.

USING THE INFORMATION

Although insiders are ultimately correct much of the time, their buying is often early. Sometimes, very early. (That's one reason some professionals don't rely on insider buying as much as they probably should. Money managers who need to turn in a monster performance this quarter frequently decide to look elsewhere for something already on the move.)

If you're going to play the insider game, you have to be patient. A stock with heavy insider buying may sit there like a lump for six months while other stocks are jumping all over the place.

You have to be prepared for this inertness—another reason it is essential to learn as much as you can about a stock before buying it. You can then feel comfortable holding it. You'll be confident that the insider's view of the company will eventually be Wall Street's as well.

YOUR STRATEGIC MOVES

The fact that insider buying doesn't immediately boost stocks is actually a great plus for the individual investor. Once you've found an intriguing insider buying situation, you have time to do the necessary research. The more research you do, the better the chance that you will make the right decision about the stock.

Step one is to get the financials and look them over. Learn enough about the company to ask some smart questions.

Then call the insider who just purchased the stock and ask what motivated him or her to buy. (*Individual Investor* includes the company's phone number for just this purpose.) Ask what's appealing about the company right now. What does the insider see that others are missing? You won't always get a complete answer, but the contact is a great way to learn.

You don't have to be a big investor or a financial journalist to enjoy this access. Any potential investor should consider calling the targeted company and asking direct questions. You'll be surprised at how much you can find out.

While you have the insider on the line, you can also ask some of the questions discussed in Chapter 2. The answers might help and they certainly couldn't hurt.

Step two is to analyze the fundamentals of the company just as you normally would. Yes, the company deserves to be regarded more highly because the insider is buying, but that doesn't make it a "buy." You still have to understand the business, the company's prospects, and its relative standing among competitors.

If insider buying is such a great indicator, why doesn't everybody use it? There are reasons. I just don't think they're particularly good ones.

- As I've said, insiders are often early. Great investors like Warren Buffett and Peter Lynch are often early, too. Over time, being early isn't a problem if you're right and if you have a long-term outlook.

- Many people think that following insiders is neither glamorous nor sexy. (Personally, I think the sex appeal comes from the results.)

- Some investors find the method too straightforward for their tastes. This is especially true of people who are determined to use investing as a forum to prove how smart they are. Piggybacking on someone else's transactions, they feel, isn't a sufficiently brilliant technique. It's too easy.

- Many investors seem to avoid doing what works. Investors often spend a great deal of time getting in their own way. They agonize over the wrong things and spend little or no time investigating the right things, the pieces of information that might actually make them money. Finding arcane reasons for buying a stock doesn't prove you're smart—unless the stock goes up.

- Insider transaction information is still not well disseminated. You have to invest a bit of effort to get it. Which means the opportunities are greater for those who do possess the information.

SPECIAL USES FOR INSIDER BUYING INFORMATION

Insider buying can help you spot small-cap stocks early, before they run up or get profiled in *The Wall Street Journal* or *The New York Times.*

You don't necessarily have to buy the stock right after learning that you like it. Often, I do not. But I do keep a list of companies that I'm watching actively. With a very young company, I may be waiting to see that first profitable quarter. Or, I may hold off until I see whether that allegedly hot new product really moves in the marketplace.

Insider activity can also lead you to turnaround situations—in fact, it's particularly effective in such cases. Once a stock has crashed and burned, people stop paying attention. Analysts begin looking elsewhere. No one expects anything good to come of this company anymore.

After a while, the only people who know what's going on at company XYZ are the folks who work there. When *they* start buying, they're sending a message that either the Street has overreacted or better times lie ahead.

A vivid example of insiders buying at the bottom occurred at Cooper Industries, a company that had the misfortune of having owned subsidiaries active in the production and distribution of silicone breast implants. Although the company had jettisoned the subsidiaries, it hadn't disposed of its legal exposure.

Cooper Industries became a lawyer's dream and a stockholder's nightmare. Shares that had once fetched more than $20 fell as low as $0.63 in late 1993.

By autumn 1993, however, scraping the bottom was history. As an investor, I'm more concerned about what's going on *now*. In October 1993, two insiders decided to buy shares in Cooper, a company that had looked as if it were on the fast track to oblivion. CFO Robert Weiss bought 100,000 shares at $0.88, and vice president Greg Fryling picked up 9,000 shares at $0.81.

The two men knew that the litigation liability was obscuring the fact that two Cooper subsidiaries, Cooper Vision and Hospital Group of America, were making money. Another subsidiary, Cooper Surgical, was also doing well. Furthermore, what the men couldn't know for certain—but probably suspected—was that most of the lawsuits would probably be settled in a manner that would allow Cooper to survive.

We spotlighted Cooper in February 1994, when it was trading at $0.63 (the two insiders were *very* early). By May, the shares had tripled to $1.88. By November, they had quadrupled to $2.50. Many of the suits were settled, and the profitable parts of Cooper kept chugging along.

Insider buying helps me in another way. It tells me that I'm probably not too late, and that's very important. Like many investors—and, probably, like you—I hate *chasing* stocks (buying them after they've had a huge move). You always have to ask yourself: Am I the last person to figure this one out? Heavy insider buying says that the people closest to the action still believe there is good news ahead.

Just be sure you always check one thing. Compare the price the insiders paid and the current stock price. If they bought two months ago at $6 and the stock is now $9.00, you may no longer be looking at a bargain. What do you do in this case? Usually, I'll wait for the stock to decline a bit before I think seriously about buying. If it doesn't fall back, then I just chalk it up to experience and move on.

Seeing insiders buy as a stock hits all-time highs is very bullish. Obviously, insiders who own the stock have a chance to sell at a profit (often an enormous percentage profit). But they are buying rather than selling. That shows a remarkable level of confidence in the future.

INSIDER SELLING

Insiders don't always buy, of course. Sometimes they sell, too.

An insider's decision to sell tells you much less than his decision to buy. People buy because they are optimistic. But there are many logical reasons to sell. Among the most common: the need to diversify one's portfolio, the understandable desire to take some profits, a major purchase (home, boat, college education), or a divorce settlement.

An investor who always sells when he encounters insider selling—who assumes it is the financial equivalent of rats fleeing a sinking ship—will live to regret it. Imagine for a moment an investor who was brilliant enough to buy Microsoft the day it went public in 1986, at a split-adjusted price of $2, but who panicked at the first insider sale.

Since the public offering, chairman Bill Gates has sold some of his holdings almost every year. In fact, he has never purchased an additional share. (Gates has used the proceeds to invest in other companies, build a home, and buy drawings by Leonardo da Vinci, among other things.)

If an investor had bailed out the first time he noticed Gates's selling, he would have exited Microsoft at a price of $9. As we went to press the stock was about ten times that price.

Despite his selling, Gates owns 160 million shares of Microsoft. I think he still has a stake in trying to make the company successful.

Gates, like many successful entrepreneurs, has instituted a personal "sell program" for a portion of his holdings. In almost every case, these programs say nothing about the executive's faith in his company.

So by itself, a little bit of insider selling doesn't bother me so much. But when I see a sustained pattern of sales, or a single huge block sold by a prominent executive, I get a little more concerned. It may cause me to look for other opportunities or reevaluate my position if I already own shares in the company. I get especially concerned when I see a sizable number of executives sharply reducing their holdings at about the same time.

I also get alarmed if insiders are selling when the stock is hitting new price lows. Who would sell shares in his own company at the lowest price the market has offered all year? Not someone who thought much of the company's future, unless he were under considerable financial strain.

I also get nervous if I see more than one high-ranking person at a company make a 144 filing. A form 144 is an SEC document filed by holders of restricted stock to provide notice of their intent to sell. Short-sellers keep a close eye on 144 filings as they search for high-fliers they hope will soon come crashing to earth. Again, if the shorts are swarming, I'd rather be elsewhere.

MY PROTECTIVE STRATEGY

Here's a technique I sometimes use to take advantage of insider buying. I'll buy a small position as soon as I've done my initial research. Once some positive numbers come through, I'll increase my holdings. If, however, the numbers don't improve as the insider buying suggests they should, I'll abandon ship.

Insiders, after all, are not always right. If they were, stock investing would be far simpler than it is. Nonetheless, your investing career will be more profitable if you recognize that insiders do have an edge. The best thing you can do is to align yourself with them rather than against them.

5

Hot Stocks

INVESTING WITH MOMENTUM

What goes up must come down, right? Right. The question is: When?

If you're a value investor who considers Graham and Dodd a sacred text, you might want to take a seasickness prevention tablet, or at least a few deep breaths, before reading this chapter. The topic: Momentum investing.

If you've ever read an article about the evils of momentum investing, I'd like you to put aside your preconceptions for a moment. Many media "experts" have dumped on momentum investing because it looks like hocus-pocus. It makes stock market profits look too easy to attain.

The fact is, momentum is a valid way to pick stocks. The general idea is to buy stocks whose prices have been rising. On its face, this technique stands in stark contrast to the traditional axiom, "Buy low, sell high." But, "low" and "high" are relative terms. A stock that has hit a new high is actually at a low if it goes still higher.

There are a number of reasons why momentum investing works, and all feed off an apparent paradox: The market is at once efficient and inefficient. What does this mean? A stock's price usually rises for a good reason—a new contract, a new product, new relationships, or maybe a positive earnings release that suggests good things to come (market efficiency). At the same time, it takes time for the market to fully incorporate news into a stock price (market inefficiency).

Over the past few years, the momentum style has gained a rising number of adherents, particularly among professional investors. As the number of momentum-oriented money managers has grown, the technique has sometimes reached ridiculous extremes, which is why the practice invites skepticism.

Merely to buy what's going up and dump what's heading down is a ludicrously simplistic way to invest money. Because the momentum players almost all tend to use the same criteria to identify stocks, they inevitably drive the prices of some stocks higher than those stocks should ever go. When they sell en masse, they beat down the prices lower than they should ever go. (This happens naturally to stock prices anyway, but the herd of momentum players exaggerates the swings and makes them occur faster.)

But the negatives of momentum investing are clearly outweighed by the positives. In fact, value investing and intelligent momentum-based strategies are actually not mutually exclusive.

The stock market tries to be efficient about how it values companies, but it is an imperfect mechanism. One reason it has to be imperfect—or, more bluntly, it has to be wrong—some of the time is that the true worth of a company can change spectacularly in the course of a week, a day, an hour, or an instant.

Let's take a crude example. Company X develops a new product. Before the item is introduced, only a few people really know how good it is. The people who worked on its development and those who tested it are aware of it, along with some managers and perhaps their colleagues or industry rivals.

Soon enough thereafter, the word starts to spread. Suppliers may learn that something is up. If the product is beta-tested, early users may get a clue. Analysts, industry gurus, and consultants may start hearing great things about it. A lot can happen before the product is ever formally announced, much less sold.

What does all this have to do with value? On the day it becomes clear that the new product actually works, the underlying value of the company that developed it might actually go up by 50%, 100%, or 300%. Some company developments are that important.

The stock market, however, seldom adjusts that quickly. (The one exception is an announcement of a takeover bid.)

What usually happens is that the stock moves up sharply but still—all things considered—trades at a discount to its new intrinsic value. A gap develops between *perceived* worth and *actual* worth. That is exactly the kind of meat that value players feed on.

Even Warren Buffett would admit this. One of the most successful investments of this legendary value player was the purchase of Coca-Cola stock in 1988. The shares had quadrupled in the previous six years. The market was coming to recognize something new about Coke.

Buffett concluded that, despite the gain, the market hadn't fully recognized what was new about Coca-Cola. So he bought $592 million worth of the stock. In the ensuing seven years, Coke shares didn't quadruple again. They rose fivefold.

There is a major stylistic difference between the two camps. Value players will run the other way when they see a stock rise 43% in three weeks. Someone interested in momentum will instead ask: Is there any sane reason that company X is worth 43% more today than it was last month?

More often than you might think, the answer is yes. Since *Individual Investor* began its momentum-based "Hot Stocks" section in early 1994, readers who bought all the stocks have enjoyed annualized average returns of 37%. The technique works, and there are solid reasons why.

In Chapter 1, I mentioned a company called PC DOCS. The stock is a perfect example of how momentum investing can sometimes be the best way to learn about the true value of a company.

If I had been a computer industry insider, I might have heard about PC DOCS years ago—but I didn't. If I had been a contented PC DOCS customer, I might have known how terrific the company was—but I didn't. If I had had a broker who specialized in small, legitimate Canadian companies worthy of a closer look . . . but, again, no such luck.

Despite all these personal shortcomings, I managed to learn about PC DOCS early enough to make a fabulous profit in the stock (as we went to press, my annualized gain was about 1,500%). You can learn about these situations, too.

We wrote about PC DOCS in March 1995, when the price was $1.94, up more than fourfold from the year's low of $0.44. Even at the loftier $1.94 price, the company's market cap was only $12.4 million. This was a very small company. It aspired to be a micro-cap. At that time, it was more like a nano-cap.

Nevertheless, PC DOCS already had some very big customers, and that excited us. What was it about this unknown Toronto company that had attracted the likes of Du Pont and Canada's Treasury Board Secretariat and Department of Finance?

We found out. PC DOCS (for *d*ocument *o*rganization and *c*ontrol *s*ystems) sells software to manage activity on complex computer networks. One of the ways to coin money in the 1990s is to make computer networks easier to run and to manage. PC DOCS was a leader in a hot market.

Was that sufficient reason to believe that the company, already a hot stock, would continue to sizzle? Absolutely not. Before I bought it, I had to be sure I knew what other people thought of the company's products, what its competitive standing was today, and what threats to market share and profitability loomed in the future.

The more independent the assessment, the more valuable the information. I was impressed when I learned that PC DOCS had won *PC Magazine*'s Editor's Choice Award for best document management software in 1991, 1993, and 1994.

I decided to learn more about the prospects for the company's niche. The Gartner Group was estimating that the market would grow ninefold between 1995 and 1997. That's a 200% annualized growth rate. Was there reason to believe that PC DOCS would get its share of that growth?

There were certainly clues. The product quality awards, for one. The satisfaction of its major customers, which could be ascertained by talking to analysts who followed PC DOCS or to the customers themselves. But, above everything else, the big clue was a new deal with Du Pont.

The Du Pont contract was the sort of event that dramatically changes the value of a small company. The deal (it was announced on January 10, 1995) explained much of the rise in PC DOCS' stock, but it was impossible for anyone to know exactly how valuable the deal would be in the long term. In that kind of uncertainty lies opportunity.

Besides adding revenue (the amount was unspecified when we wrote about the deal), the Du Pont coup put PC DOCS into another league. Why was an American giant with 114,000 employees relying on an obscure Canadian company? It certainly wasn't for prestige. The client liked the product and felt that PC DOCS had the expertise to service its enormous needs. It was a good bet that other American and Canadian companies would reach similar conclusions.

In fact, this predictable phenomenon helps explain why hot stocks so often become hotter. One success has a habit of leading to others and makes it easier to persuade potential customers to sign up and test a product. (When an independent party ranks your product number one, it's reasonable to assume that many who try it will also find it superior.)

The value of the Du Pont deal wasn't just in the revenue stream per se, important though that was. The deal solidified PC DOCS' leadership position in an industry that was growing at a phenomenal rate. I've seen this same story play out countless times, usually with technology companies.

It starts with a trigger event, often a new contract or new product. The market responds to the event—but it usually underreacts. That sets up the classic hot stock opportunity for investors. (Another appealing aspect of the story: In April 1994, PC DOCS' chairman bought 649,998 shares of his company on the open market.)

Don't expect every momentum play to be as picture-perfect as PC DOCS. What happened next was truly remarkable. Our subscribers got the PC DOCS article about February 20, 1995. On February 27, PC DOCS announced a major mutual sales accord with

Wang Laboratories. Wang isn't the powerhouse it used to be, but it's still a billion-dollar company with a large customer base. The deal could only help. The stock rose 10% on the news.

On March 8, PC DOCS reported that it had won another important contract, this time with the General Accounting Office of the United States. The stock rose another 15%.

On March 29, the company announced the introduction of a new document management/production imaging product. The stock rose again, but by this point it was rising almost every day, whether the company made an announcement or not.

On April 20, PC DOCS announced that it had won yet another award: first place in the Buyers' Satisfaction Scorecard in *Computer-World* magazine's "Guide to Document Management."

Just five days later, on April 25, the company released earnings for the quarter ended March 31. They were tremendous. Sales were up 92% to $9.6 million (U.S.) and the company earned $1.47 million (U.S.)—12 cents a share compared to a loss the previous year of a penny per share.

The stock rose another 13% on the news.

All in all, in fewer than four months after our article appeared, the shares had gone from $1.94 to $11.38, a gain of 487%.

WHY THE APPROACH WORKS

Every investor knows the phrase, "Buy low, sell high." It's a nice enough phrase—one of my favorites, in fact.

But that's not the only way to make money in the market. Another great maxim is, "Buy high, sell higher."

According to financial newsletter expert Mark Hulbert, three of the top long-term performers among newsletter writers use this variation of relative-strength investing. Louis Navellier of *MPT Review*, Dan Sullivan of *The Chartist*, and James Collins of *OTC Insight* have made big money for their subscribers by concluding that strong stocks have a curious habit of getting stronger.

Here's why the approach works so well so often.

- As I've already discussed, it takes a lot of time for the market to assess the full impact of really good corporate news.

- Companies go on winning streaks—and losing streaks as well. Success is contagious. So is failure. Some of this is based on reality, some on perception. They're both important.

As an example, let's return to IBM. I couldn't have told you that IBM would fall from a high of $170 in 1987 to a low of $40 in 1993, but, as the stock became unglued, I would have told you to avoid it at almost any price until there was a reason for buying it again.

Why? Because IBM wasn't just losing market share and hemorraghing money. The company had become a loser. Its reputation for technological innovation and price performance was atrocious, and deservedly so. Propeller heads—the people who know the most about technology and help determine what's hot and what's not—had nothing but contempt for the company. The smartest college graduates didn't want to go near it.

IBM had become a bad technology company that was living off its reputation for service and its huge installed base. Unless both the reality and the perception changed, IBM didn't have a prayer of becoming a great company or a great stock. Keep in mind:

- Stock prices always rise for a reason—often, a good reason. Price action can lead you to stocks that are poised for future gains.

- The cost of owning a stock that is not hot may be greater than you think.

There are several kinds of losers. Holding a stock whose price remains stagnant for years is a very expensive proposition. It doesn't matter that the stock hasn't dropped; what's key is that it hasn't risen in price while other potential investments have appreciated. This kind of stock is called dead money. If you have too many examples in your portfolio at any one time, they can kill your performance.

Besides taking a toll on your psyche, dead money stocks painfully illustrate the importance of *opportunity cost:* If your money weren't locked up in a dud, it would be earning a reasonable rate of return elsewhere. Let's do some dead money math.

You buy 100 shares of Bow-Wow Industries (ticker symbol: DOG) at $20. Your commission fee is $50. Three years later, the stock is still $20 and you decide to sell, again paying a $50 commission.

You're out $100 in commissions on a $2,000 investment, for a total loss of $100, right?

Wrong.

You've also lost the money you would have made if you had chosen a more lucrative investment. For simplicity's sake, let's assume you had put the money in a stock or fund that rose 10% per year, the market's historic rate of return. By not doing that, you lost 10% a year for three years. Factoring in the benefits of compounding—which you, of course, missed out on—you actually lost 32% over three years. Now add in the commission cost.

The good news is that, for three years, you owned a stock that didn't decline. Things could have been worse. The bad news is that your investment choice cost you real money in excess of the commission.

If you're looking to find the big winners in the stock market, there's only one place they all have to show up. They may never appear on the new lows list (often, they will spend years without ever hitting that list), but the top performers inevitably appear on the new highs list—when they go, say from $2 to $20.

The trick, obviously, is to buy a stock closer to $2 than to $20.

PROBLEMS WITH THE METHOD

The first problem investors have with the momentum style is that it takes intestinal fortitude to buy a stock at $10 today when you know that it was selling for $6 four months ago.

Knowing it could have been bought at a cheaper price never makes anyone feel good. ("If I can't get it cheap, I don't want it at all" is a common investor dictum. But, except for the world's great value investors, it's not a very profitable stance for most people.) And, you're smart enough to know that a stock that just rose 67% or 150% or 250% in the past year might reverse direction and go into a free fall. There are, after all, things worse than dead money. One of them is no money.

Like most difficult things in investing, this approach gets easier over time. It only takes a success or two before you realize that a stock's phenomenal performance in the six months or year before you discovered it does nothing to invalidate reasons for purchasing today, especially if you employ the same analytical criteria that you normally do.

Consider the stock of Alpha Industries. The Massachusetts-based company had a market cap of $46.1 million when *Individual Investor* recommended it in November 1994. Six months before, however, its market cap had been $23 million. By the time we noticed the stock, it had already doubled from its yearly low. That would be enough to scare some people away.

A closer look revealed that Alpha was still undervalued. It was a classic turnaround story of a military contractor diversifying into wireless communications products. The trigger for the recent stock price rise? A $20 million contract from Motorola to make ceramic duplexer filters that block unwanted signals over cellular phones.

That was wonderful news on several fronts. The quality and importance of the customer were obvious. If you're going to win a new contract in the cellular phone business, you can't do better than Motorola.

The size of the contract was also a major positive. Alpha's total revenues in the previous year were $70 million, so a $20 million deal was enormously important. If nothing else happened immediately, that by itself would have a big impact on earnings. And it was a very clear indication that Alpha's new corporate direction seemed to be viable.

Actually, even before the Motorola deal, our research showed that Alpha's new strategy was working. Wireless communications sales constituted 44% of total revenues in 1994, up from just 17% in 1993. After the thunderclap of the Motorola announcement, there was more good news: stronger earnings, new analyst coverage, and a recommendation in *Barron's* in February 1995. Alpha shares, which had doubled in the previous months, doubled again in the following six months, getting as high as $14.25 in April 1995, a gain of 138%.

Although I wouldn't characterize owning a hot stock as a fling, it is seldom a marriage either. Usually, you'll want to own these stocks for six months, a year, or two years, but seldom much longer. Although winning streaks tend to persist, they do not last forever.

From a tax standpoint, then, this is not an ideal situation, unless you own these stocks in a tax-sheltered account. As Warren Buffett has so lucidly pointed out, and so brilliantly illustrated in his investing career, it is far better to make 20% a year on a stock you never sell than to make 20% this year on stock A, 20% next year on stock B, 20% the year after on stock C, and so on. The tax consequences of taking a profit can be staggering.

Another negative about this group of stocks is that they tend to be volatile. We first noticed them because they were going higher faster than their peers. When they fall, they often fall faster as well.

Remember Clearly Canadian? The stock ran from $1.44 all the way up to $26.13 in 1991. Six months later, the stock was $10. By 1994, it was as low as $1.06.

If you're going to try this approach, you have to be disciplined and you can't be too greedy. The punishment for overstaying your welcome can be brutal.

GETTING IN AND GETTING OUT: A STRATEGY

The best way to begin making money through momentum investing is to start with the knowledge that not every hot stock stays hot. Some have a brief moment of glory and then turn into boring laggards that can diminish returns and frustrate a patient investor. Others soar solo for a while, only to plunge when they run into competitors, or changing industry fundamentals, or sharp-eyed auditors.

Then there are stocks like Proxima Corporation. Proxima manufactures LCD-based desktop projection products, which have helped revolutionize the audio/visual industry. Its projectors and panel systems are regularly used for business meetings and computer-based presentations.

When we wrote about Proxima in 1994, it was trading at $11.75 and had a market cap of $73.8 million. During the next six months, Proxima announced new marketing agreements with the likes of Texas Instruments, and two remarkable earnings reports. On July 26, it announced that first quarter net was $0.36 a share, compared to a year-earlier loss of $0.02 a share.

Three months later, the news was that second quarter net more than doubled: $0.45 a share versus $0.20. The earnings were well above the most optimistic analyst's projections. By mid-November 1994, Proxima shares had more than tripled, rising as high as $39.63.

But, six weeks later, this extraordinarily volatile stock was back to $30, a 25% retreat in the blink of an eye. (Some hot stock, its holders must have muttered.) Then it went up again.

On May 2, 1995, Proxima reported another quarter of tremendous earnings (56 cents versus 23 cents), but cautioned that it might experience an earnings and revenue "slowness" in the current quarter because of competition and the production ramp-up of its Desktop Projector 5100. The market reacted savagely, slashing Proxima's stock price from $33.38 to $27.13, a drop of 19%. Two days later, the stock was $24.

I have a rule about volatile stocks. It's not an absolute rule, but I usually follow it. When a stock moves so far so fast, I think it's smart to sell part of the stake—ideally, an amount equal to the original cost of entry. If the stock has doubled, selling half the stake accomplishes this. If it has tripled, sell one-third of the holdings.

Psychologically, one of the most powerful things you can do with a volatile stock is, in the argot of Las Vegas, play with the house's money. In that way, you can feel confident that you won't be shaken out by inevitable price gyrations. Almost paradoxically, selling some of your stake actually makes it easier to hold the rest of your stock for the long haul.

This still doesn't mean you hold on forever if the fundamentals of the business change radically. "The house's money" is just a phrase, after all. The money is really yours. You earned it. It's real. Don't fritter it away.

I don't follow my rule all the time. Sometimes, one of my stocks doubles and I'll buy more rather than sell. Or perhaps I'll just hold what I have. Or, I'll sell the entire position and go elsewhere.

The newer you are at these decisions, the more important it is to stick to my rule. In any case, your decision should be based on careful research into the stock's fundamentals and your own determination that the stock is—at this moment—undervalued, overvalued, or fairly priced.

Sometimes, you might be too busy to research a stock, or you might realize that the true value of the company is really unknowable at this point in its history. (This is most likely to be true for a company awaiting government approval to market a product.) When in doubt, follow the rule.

Where to Find Hot Stocks

One way or another, you should screen the new highs list (a comprehensive roster is published in *Barron's* every week). The problem is, there's an embarrassment of riches.

On each trading day in 1994, for instance, approximately 150 stocks hit new highs. On some days, the total reached 500. You can't perform due diligence on all of them. But there are some good ways to narrow the field.

- Use *Investor's Business Daily.* Stocks hitting new highs are frequently highlighted in the paper's editorial columns. In addition, graphs of as many as 50 stocks reaching new highs are featured each day. These charts include information on the companies' business, market capitalization, recent earnings history, and relative strength.

- When reading about the stock market in any publication, pay particular attention to discussions of stocks making new highs. Mark down the names of companies you want to learn more about.

- Use software to analyze the prospects of various strong stocks. Example: You could run a screen on recent new highs to find stocks with the most appealing PEG ratios, based on next year's estimated earnings. (The PEG ratio is the stock's P/E ratio divided by its earnings growth rate.)

- Use *Individual Investor*. Every issue features a "Hot Stocks" section, with graphs, data, and analysis on about ten companies that seem to be making new highs for the right reasons.

No matter what resources you're using, taking a momentum-based approach can help you identify hot industries. In preparing our "Hot Stocks" section, we've been struck at how often an industry represented in, say, June, will also appear in July, August, and October. Something like this recently happened with semiconductor makers, semiconductor equipment companies, and bar code scanning companies.

Call this Cockroach Theory, part two. When a few stocks from the same group appear in your momentum research, the chances are good that a similar company will join them soon. This possibility can help influence your buying decisions.

For example, you've been eyeing a chipmaker that has experienced strong insider buying. Several other semiconductor companies are starting to set new highs, although the one you're watching hasn't done so yet. All things being equal, you've got good signs that the industry is hot—another reason to consider buying the stock rather than waiting six months.

SEPARATING WHEAT FROM CHAFF

A new high is nice, but by itself it isn't enough to justify a financial commitment. Here are some of the reasons I might avoid investing in a stock that just hit a new high:

- An extremely lofty P/E ratio based on next year's earnings.

- A very high price/sales ratio (an exception might be made for a development stage company or one that has just begun selling products).

- An astronomical price/book ratio.

- A recent initial public offering (IPO). There are two problems here. The first is simple: It's easier for a stock that has been trading for only a month or two to make the new highs list. Second, IPOs often rise quickly soon after trading begins, as underwriters help support the price and institutions scramble to get shares, often at silly levels.

Sometimes, I think IPO really stands for *initial price orbit.* Then, alas, the prices of the stocks usually come crashing back to earth. The upshot: Usually, the initial price performance of the fledgling public company doesn't say much about the long-term value of the company. In fact, if I had to buy a recent IPO, I'd prefer to buy one that was flat or down rather than up sharply.

Here are the right reasons to get excited about a stock making a new high:

- A positive earnings surprise.

- Rapidly growing earnings.

- A large order from a new, and respected, customer.

- Expanding profit margins.

- An exciting new product.

- A strong position in a rapidly growing niche business.

- A major trend that is boosting sales.

- A significant corporate restructuring (spinoff, divestiture, cost-cutting, and so on).

- A new marketing alliance or an important acquisition. For a small company, a single acquisition can be profoundly important. It may open up new markets or allow the company to profit from genuine economies of scale for the first time. Be especially alert for a smart small company that buys a moderate-sized division from a Fortune 500 company. In the right hands, such deals often turn out to be strategically brilliant.

  The reasons aren't mysterious. The big company's main goal may be to unload the division, which is quite possibly a money loser and, at best, no longer a strategic asset. Its negotiating team may not go through contortions to get top dollar. (After all, at a $10 billion company, $10 million is a rounding error.) The small company, on the other hand, will either make the deal on its terms or walk away.

  Small is not only beautiful. It's often powerful as well.

- The initiation of coverage by a major analyst. (If the analyst works for an investment banker who recently brought the company public, disregard the recommendation. In such cases, the endorsement is mere boilerplate. Unfortunately, that's how business is done on Wall Street.)

- A management shakeup (if—and only if—the new top people are known quantities in the particular industry).

Here are some examples to show you how the process works and suggest its enormous profit potential.

New Product/Key Acquisition/Analyst Recommendation

The Key Tronic story shows that, even when it comes to hot stocks, patience can be a virtue. Many of our hot stock successes double pretty fast, but it's unreasonable to conclude that if a stock doesn't turn in this kind of sizzling performance it's a dud. Stocks may need to consolidate the gains that originally attracted investors, as Key Tronic did.

We recommended the Spokane-based company in November 1994. The news on the company was terrific: there were three good reasons for the stock to keep rising.

1. It had just collaborated with Microsoft to make an enhanced ergonomic keyboard to be used with Windows 95. The Natural Keyboard is more user-friendly, has more keys, and enables a user to activate more functions with a keystroke. Its unusual design is also supposed to reduce the incidence of repetitive stress injuries so common among heavy computer users.

2. Key Tronic had recently acquired Honeywell's keyboard manufacturing plant in Mexico.

3. Piper Jaffray analyst Robert Toomey, impressed by the company's cost advantages over Asian competitors, had issued a buy recommendation.

The stock was $10.38, up from a year low of $5.75, when we recommended it.

However, for months after our story appeared, the stock hardly budged. Then, after announcing solid earnings, it began a slow and steady climb. Key Tronic reported that it would produce a special keyboard for IBM's new laptop, the first full-size keyboard ever to fit into a subnotebook. Its new CEO, turnaround specialist Stanley Hiller, had shown his faith in the company by building a 30% equity stake.

Soon thereafter, the stock hit $15.25, a gain of 47%. Less spectacular than some of the other gains discussed in this chapter, granted; but a very nice move for a six-month holding period.

Anyone convinced that this hot stock had to lead to a quick buck, however, would have been disappointed and probably would have sold too soon.

A Large New Order

In February 1995, we wrote about the stock of Genus, a producer of semiconductor manufacturing equipment. Genus's stock, then $7.31, had already doubled from its mid-1994 low. But a new sale it had just announced was indeed impressive. The world's largest maker of computer memory chips, Samsung Electronics, had ordered $22 million worth of Genus equipment. On a percentage basis, this was far more meaningful than Alpha's Motorola coup, because, in 1993, Genus's total sales were just $44.2 million.

When a new order is so large, good things tend to happen to stock prices. Within three months, Genus had hit $11.63, a gain of an additional 59%.

Hot Industry/Divestiture

The elimination of a poorly performing division can help light a rocket under a stock. It's essential that the businesses the company keeps are performing well and have reason to improve in the near future.

When we wrote about Peak Technology in July 1994, the New York City company was trading at $11.88 and had a market cap of $64 million. Peak is in a great business. It makes bar codes for industry. Companies use them to keep up-to-the-minute tabs on inventory.

Late in 1993, the company eliminated its data storage division, for two reasons: (1) it was unprofitable and (2) the money spent on the division could clearly be used to generate big profits in the bar code business.

The results Peak reported for the quarter right before our recommendation suggested the strategy was working. Revenues rose 43% to $25.6 million—a wonderful number, considering that the company had just eliminated a division—and earnings were up a spectacular 250% to 7 cents a share.

Earnings reports for the next four quarters were also terrific: $0.16 versus $0.10; $0.22 versus $0.15; $0.26 versus a loss of $1.01; and $0.16 versus $0.07, respectively.

The stock rose steadily and peaked at $21.25 in March 1995, up 79% from the recommended price.

New Marketing/Product Development Alliance

Stratacom, one of the great stocks of the 1990s and a darling of small-cap fund managers, has been featured in our "America's Fastest Growing Companies" section several times. That's what happens when a company finds a way to double its earnings quarter after quarter. But we had recommended Stratacom in our "Hot Stocks" section before some of those spectacular earnings gains came through. Readers had a chance to grab the stock at $22 in June 1994.

Again, we were hardly early. The company already had a market cap of $700 million. But we were excited by the earnings story (the latest quarter had been up 50%), the recent stock price run-up, and, in particular, a new product development and marketing alliance that had the industry buzzing.

Stratacom's stock was rising partly because it had just announced an agreement with Synoptics to develop technology to allow customers to connect local-area and wide-area Asynchronous Transfer Mode networks (ATMs). ATMs are an extraordinarily important technology because they allow faster communication of data, voice, and video.

By March 1995, after reporting a quarterly earnings gain of 300%, Stratacom hit $47, a gain of 114% in less than a year.

Hot New Product

It was hard to buy Xylogics, but it would have been unfortunate to avoid the stock. Xylogics proves that jumping in after a stock has had a powerful vertical move can still make you a lot of money.

We wrote about it in our December 1994 issue. The stock had just had a good month before we were smart enough to cover it: It had risen 75% in 30 days. Nice work if you can get it.

At its new and improved price of $13.38, the company had a market cap of $68 million. The two essential questions now were: (1) Was the move justified? (2) Had the new realities about the company been fully factored in? The answers were yes and no, respectively.

Xylogics manufactures communication and terminal server networking products, which allow users to access servers via PCs from almost anywhere. Its stock spiked after the company announced Annex Release 9.0, an enhanced version of its remote access servers. The industry and analyst response was enthusiastic.

Xylogics was already a very strong player in a market that was likely to reach $1 billion in annual sales by 1998. Already, there were more than 25 million mobile users who could benefit from this kind of communications product.

Conversations with analysts helped convince us that this strong niche company in a fast-growing market was still significantly undervalued, even after its recent price rise. Why? Because Xylogics was trading for only 15 times its estimated earnings for the fiscal year ending October 1995. That's not an appropriate multiple for a market leader that is growing so rapidly in an attractive niche. (At the time, the average stock in the S&P 500 was selling at 16 times next year's earnings.) Xylogics was still being mispriced by the market.

Three weeks after our recommendation, the company reported a 78% rise in quarterly income. The next quarter, earnings grew 54%. Within four months of the writeup, the stock had jumped to $28, a gain of 102%.

New Product/Attractive Acquisition

A hot new product and a smart acquisition made us decide that Softkey, at a price of $17.50, looked like a winner in December 1994. Within four months, the stock was $29.13.

Softkey was already a substantial company, with a market cap of $210 million. It was tied with better-known Broderbund for the lead in the U.S. consumer software market. We liked the market and were impressed by Softkey's leadership position.

The company's new product? Don't blame us, but it was a CD-ROM version of the *Sports Illustrated* swimsuit calendar, the best-selling calendar in America. With this software, consumers would now—for the first time—be able to create custom calendars and datebooks featuring the swimsuit models. (Our long-suffering staff spent hours analyzing the software before we saw fit to recommend the stock.)

Softkey's acquisition was more high-minded. It made a strong entrance into multimedia "edutainment" by purchasing Software Marketing Corporation, a company whose 1993 sales were $4.7 million. The deal added fourteen software titles to SoftKey's 170-title library.

It would have been hard for an investor to find out about SoftKey by focusing on earnings. For its last fiscal year, there weren't any. The company was just about to become profitable when the recent spike in its shares brought it to our attention. But the earnings projections were great. We felt the shares represented a bargain even though they had recently run up on the good news.

If the company matched the consensus analyst estimates of $1.25 per share for the fiscal year ending in June 1995, it was selling for a P/E ratio of just 14. For a fast-growing leader in a red-hot industry, that's dirt cheap.

In fact, if you've never tried momentum investing before, this kind of projected P/E ratio could provide the comfort factor you need to get your feet wet. A company selling for a below-market multiple can hardly be called a high flier in the pejorative sense of the term. (After all, its P/E ratio was lower than that of blue chips such as Procter & Gamble, 3M, and McDonald's.) But when a company has a growth rate of 50% and a projected P/E ratio of 14, there's a lot of upside potential. There's downside protection as well. The growth rate could decline by 25%, or even 50%, and the stock would still be a sensible purchase.

A Niche Play

We first wrote about Supertex, the tiny Sunnyvale, California, semiconductor company, in April 1994, when its stock was $3.75 and its market cap was $44.5 million. We liked the story so much that we made Supertex a 1995 Magic 25 selection.

We learned about the company primarily because we were focusing on a seemingly unrelated industry. After becoming excited about the flat-panel display business, we wrote articles on Plasma Therm and Planar. As it turned out, both used Supertex semiconductors.

This is exactly the kind of unexpected tidbit that can prove immensely valuable. Find a fast-growing business and then locate a little-known but absolutely essential supplier of a noncommodity product, and you have a recipe for a stock market winner—often, an enormous winner.

Flat-panel display makers need Supertex semiconductors because their complicated design allows the chips to withstand extreme electrical voltage. Chips found in the display panels of a jet fighter cockpit, for example, must be able to tolerate jolts of more than 100 volts of electricity. By contrast, a PC microprocessor needs to withstand only 5 volts.

We also liked the fact that Supertex was already profitable—it did well in other attractive niches such as the ultrasound machine and inkjet printer markets—and was selling for only 15 times estimated 1994 earnings. The market was starting to bid up its share price, and we saw that as confirmation that we were on to something. Indeed we were.

In the year after our recommendation, the flat-panel display market continued to grow rapidly, and Supertex produced quarter after quarter of impressive earnings. By March 1995, the stock reached $9.63, an eleven-month gain of 157%.

Major Trend

Momentum analysis helped us capitalize on the semiconductor industry's hot streak in another way. In the process, I learned something about photomasks.

Photomasks are photographic quartz plates that contain images of electronic circuits. If you want to make semiconductors, you can't live without them. Du Pont shares 80% of the photomask market with a small company called Photronics.

From trough to peak, Photronics was up 40% in the first quarter of 1994. A nice gain, but it was well behind the 75% revenue rise and 68% earnings increase in the company's most recent quarter. That gap suggested there might be more profit potential here.

As the chip industry continued to boom, Photronics reported quarter after quarter of stunning results. The stock, adjusted for a split, hit $24.83 in 1995, a gain of 173%. There were many other ways to play the semiconductor cycle during this period, but Photronics proved to be one of the better ones.

New Analyst Coverage

Momentum investing sometimes leads to turnarounds before terrific earnings comparisons are apparent for all to see. Frame Technology, for example, had a terrible 1993. The developer of software for the publishing of professional and technical documents suffered a dramatic decline in sales and lost a whopping $2.52 a share in 1993. That's quite a hit.

Despite the bad year, it remained a substantial company, with top-drawer customers such as Citibank, Boeing, Saab, and Ford Motor. The customer list was big plus. Frame's market cap at the time was $159 million.

The stock's recent price rise attracted us—it had just risen from $9 to $12—and the action of a respected analyst at a leading brokerage impressed us enough to write about it in June 1994. Mary McCaffrey of Alex. Brown initiated coverage of Frame with a buy recommendation. Convinced that the company had successfully restructured, she forecast earnings of $0.40 for 1994 and $0.60 for 1995. She was particularly enthusiastic about Frame's entry into the Windows market.

We read her report, talked to the company and to other analysts, and generally liked what we learned. Positive earnings reports soon began to flow. In April 1995, Frame reported yet another standout quarter, with net income of $0.22 a share, up from $0.10. The stock reached $22.25, a gain of 105%.

Corporate Restructuring

Emulex proves just how far a truly hot stock can go. In the spring of 1994, it hit a low of $3.13. In November, we featured the stock. Unfortunately, the shares had already rocketed to $9.75. Too late?

Hardly. Emulex, which had emerged from a restructuring the previous year, was riding the networking wave. It manufactures identification cards for the backs of printers, and wide area network cards that allow information to be processed without bogging down an entire system. After our story appeared, analysts repeatedly raised earnings estimates, and trade magazines started writing about the company's enhanced standing in the industry.

By May 1995, the stock had reached $21.63, a 122% gain on top of the 211% gain that we had been unable to catch.

Another Niche

When volatile momentum plays show signs of faltering, you should bail out faster than you normally would. Be vigilant about locking in profits. But that doesn't mean you should trash your standard analytical techniques and abandon a hot stock as soon as it shows the first signs of cooling down.

That approach would have been a definite mistake with Encad, maker of the large-format, high-resolution $7,500 Novajet color printer for the professional design market. We recommended Encad in April 1994 at $9.88. At the time, the San Diego company had a market cap of $54.3 million and was competing successfully against giant Hewlett-Packard (H-P), which had a market cap of $30 billion.

Actually, Encad was competing by concentrating on a niche that H-P was ignoring—the CAD/CAM printer market. Encad doubled to $19.75 by September, but there were some problems that put pressure on the stock.

H-P had filed a patent infringement suit against Encad the previous summer, and some investors worried about the implications. Next, the company was a month late introducing its cheaper Cadjet model, targeted at lower-end computer design firms. Finally, one of its largest distributors reported a shortfall in orders.

In a flash, the stock was hammered down below $13. We did intensive follow-up research and came to the conclusion that the suit would ultimately be dismissed and that the Cadjet delay had no long-term significance. It would lead to a one-time earnings shortfall of a few cents a share. (This was precisely the kind of bad corporate news that sometimes creates a buying opportunity. It happened with Microsoft in 1995, when the company announced that Windows 95 would be a few months late. The stock drooped, then soared.)

The decline in business reported by the distributor was already being more than made up by new distribution agreements. So, before dumping Encad, a prudent investor would ask: What is the company worth today?

Here was a company with a 30% growth rate selling at a mouth-watering valuation: 11.8 times 1994 earnings, and 8.2 times 1995 estimates. If you believe in PEG ratios, as I do, that spells opportunity. We advised readers to accumulate more shares at $13.

We hope they did, because the good news on Encad once again began flowing. The H-P suit was settled in late January 1995, just a week after our repeat buy recommendation reached readers. Then came the blowout quarter reported on April 21. Earnings soared to $0.36 a share from $0.19, on a 70% gain in revenues.

Investor psychology turned around. The shares rose 30% in a week, hitting $26.25 by May 1995, up 166% from the company's "Hot Stocks" appearance and 102% from our reiterated buy recommendation just two months before.

CONCLUSION

Despite some excesses by momentum players, momentum investing is not just a gimmick or a fad. Don't believe everything you read about it.

The best performers in the stock market will always be hot stocks at some point in their life cycle. Wal-Mart, McDonald's,

Coca-Cola, and Home Depot are just a few we could point to. The fact that a stock is hot is not an automatic endorsement, but it may be a valuable clue that something significant is going on.

As long as you continue to apply your normal valuation standards, investing in hot stocks rather than cool ones can give you an advantage. If you're still dubious, consider the opposite of momentum investing. Suppose you met someone who told you that he or she never bought shares in a company that was doing well. Why not? Because it was doing well. This person wanted to find companies whose stocks were swooning or treading water.

Yes, some people can make money that way, but, in my personal opinion, the idea of setting up a system that excludes fast-growing, thriving companies with great potential seems absurd. You can make more money with a different approach.

6

Making the Trend
Your Friend

HOW TO PROFIT FROM
THEMES AND SECTORS

Every investor is prone to the "I should have known" blues, the absolute knowledge—after the fact—that a stock or group of stocks would soar.

I know two cures for the feeling. One is to take a deep breath and then concentrate on searching for the stocks that look most attractive *today*. The other is to have purchased the stock or stocks in the first place.

The fact is, you can make a surprising amount of money by recognizing and understanding major trends and themes. The most valuable information on big trends is usually right there in front of your nose—in newspapers, magazines, and trade journals, or on television. You can even find it on the streets of your neighborhood.

Some trends are so obvious that many people assume they cannot possibly have any real-world value. Consider the dramatic changes in human longevity. This fact has been discussed now for almost two decades, as has its obvious investment implication: Buy health care stocks. It is common knowledge and old news to say that we're all living longer.

In fact, it is so common an observation that all the money that could have been made on it must be long gone by now, right? Not quite. Despite a sharp pullback while the national health care proposals were being debated in Congress, the health care sector has dramatically outperformed the entire stock market since the early 1980s. Following the decimation of the Clinton health reform, the segment has soared again.

In other words, despite its being widely known, the underlying trend is getting stronger. That doesn't mean that throwing darts at a list of health care stocks will improve your returns. But this sector is a great place to search for winners.

FINDING THE RIGHT THEMES

To find the right themes, try to look at the news from a slightly different perspective. Be alert for opportunities.

They can come from:

- Demographic changes. The health care story is, first and foremost, a tale of an aging population and the items and services older people spend their money on.

- Shifting industry perceptions. The trend toward improved quality by U.S. automakers in the 1980s was widely reported, even outside of the regular business press.

- New technology. The list is long, but it includes medical gizmos, computer networking, and the Internet.

- New business practices. The move toward outsourcing and hiring more temporary workers clearly benefits some well-positioned companies.

- Industry consolidation. The gobbling up of regional banks is one of the great examples of the 1990s' urge to merge.

- New legislation. In 1995, the Federal Communications Commission raised the limit on the number of radio stations companies could own. The investment fallout was hardly shocking: In the next few months, dozens of radio mergers took place, and the radio station group as a whole outperformed the rest of the stock market. (In case you're wondering, I missed out on this play entirely.)

When looking for a theme to ride, play into your own strengths. What business do you know? What is happening at work that might give you an early clue about what's happening elsewhere in American commerce? Do you have firsthand knowledge of a new technology?

Once you zero in on themes that interest you, seek out more detailed information. The goal is not to become an expert in every investment area that interests you—life's too short for that, even if you're an information junkie like me—but it is to understand enough so that you can successfully ride an emerging wave. Daily newspapers can be helpful, but they are often insufficient. Trade publications can be extraordinarily useful. You don't have to read every issue of each magazine covering a particular sector, but if you look at one or two occasionally you'll definitely get a better sense of which companies are leading and which are lagging.

Sometimes, books can help. Last year, I gave everyone on my staff, as well as some friends, a copy of Nicholas Negroponte's *Being Digital*. Interestingly, this book by the founding director of the MIT Media Lab is not an investment guide at all. But it explains technological trends so well that most readers will start to wonder: Who will benefit from development X, Y, and Z?

The book, together with conversations with other sources, has already affected my investment life. In a world that's being digitized quickly, some once-promising technologies are already dinosaurs.

One possible innovation could be digitized TV, which will allow so many new technologies to flourish that viewers will pay up for exciting new opportunities. Example: Not too long from now, you'll probably be able to view a sporting event from any seat in the stadium or from the perspective of the ball or a particular participant. Will people pay a little more to take advantage of this? I think so. As a result, televisions will need new equipment to handle the new technology.

One of the best companies in this business right now is Wegener Corporation, which manufactures digital audio transmitters and receivers. (We recommended Wegener in our *Special Situation Report* in January 1996.) The companies that help consumers access these new possibilities will make a fortune. Wegener should be one of them, but it may not be, which brings up another advantage of paying attention to trade journals. The trades are often where you catch the first inkling that someone has come along with a technology that is better than that of the company you have backed.

Realizing the implications of a trend clearly enough—and early enough—can help make you a great investor. Many of the sharpest business minds in America made their fortunes because they had an insight that a single development would change the world. When young Bill Gates read about the first personal computer in *Popular Mechanics*, he is famously said to have understood that the PC would inevitably doom Big Blue's mainframe business.

IBM's ultimate survival is not the point here. It is that Gates immediately figured out that the existence of one little machine would change the paradigm of computing forever.

Story Stocks?

Does the digital TV scenario make Wegener a "story stock"? I don't think so, but let's examine the term for a moment.

"Story stock" is a term often used to describe a company that might have found a cure for cancer or invented a pill that allows you to eat nothing but potato chips and yet become a mountain of bulging muscle. Trouble is, the wonderful hopes almost never become reality. With hindsight, most investors realize that there was never much evidence that made the story convincing. It was just a good tale.

When you're looking for new trends to invest in, you will always run into some stocks like these. My advice is to avoid them in favor of companies with stories that are at least half-written. Wegener, for example, is already profitable, a good sign that the company's prospects are not pure pie in the sky. You should also look for third-party confirmation—customers, patients, scientists, and companies that have used the miracle product and found that it actually works in the real world.

Too Late to the Party?

One reason investors don't take advantage of exciting themes as often as they should is that they are afraid they'll jump in precisely when the trend is peaking. In most cases, this concern is overblown. The best trends to follow are those that clearly have sufficient momentum to last for many years, if not decades.

Consider the following examples:

- The population will continue to get older.
- Whether computer sales boom or not, networking sales will remain robust.
- The medical community will embrace devices that are more cost-efficient and less invasive for the patient.
- The Internet will become an enormous business.

Just because a category will experience spectacular growth doesn't mean that an individual stock is worth buying. The overall trend may remain intact, but if you own stock in a company with a stratospheric valuation, you are starting with a tremendous handicap. You may indeed be on time for the party but too late to sample this particular dish.

The first step in your analysis should be to assess the longevity and vitality of the investment theme. I don't care if you're talking about the Internet or the U.S. auto business; the point is to understand the dynamics of the industry. What is driving growth? What customer needs are being met? What looming competition might bring this trend to an abrupt halt? How much of the theme seems like hype?

Perhaps most important: Get a sense of the time frame of a particular thematic concept. How long will it take before potential can become reality? And just how inevitable is the trend? For example, the aging of the populace is demographically indisputable. Digital TV, on the other hand, may be probable but some heretofore unknown technology might supplant it before it even gets a chance to take off.

Perform due diligence on a group just as you would on an individual stock. Get growth assumptions from analysts, talk to companies in the field, and read stories in the business press and in trade magazines. When you talk to company officials, try to establish a rapport that will allow you to talk to them more than once. They can be surprisingly good resources. Directly or indirectly, they can lead you to related investing ideas and opportunities.

In addition, consider reading annual reports issued by some of the field's leaders. Be sure you understand potential competitive threats that could quickly make a trend irrelevant.

Once you have confidence that a theme is worth your investment, is it time to start looking for specific stocks? Perhaps not. There are more conservative ways to play attractive themes. Mutual funds, for example, may be the best way for the average investor to profit from the biotech revolution. Similarly, a regional bank fund makes great sense for someone who is convinced that banking consolidation will continue but is not sure which individual banks will participate.

WORKING BACKWARD TO FIND THE RIGHT STOCKS

Well before Netscape went public in 1995, we concluded that the Internet was a terrific theme to play. To us, it wasn't just a great business opportunity. It was also an important new aspect of the rapidly digitizing world. The next steps were to read more about the Internet, seeking profitable ways to play it, and to find Internet companies and learn what they did.

What led us to CMG Information Services (CMGI)? First, it was a value play. In December, the company had sold its PC-based viewer/browser Internet technology to America Online (AOL) for 1.4 million AOL shares, then valued at $30 million. As AOL's stock raced ahead, CMGI shares did not keep pace, proving that even in an area as hot as the Internet, it is possible to find a bargain.

CMGI represented far more than a cheap way to invest in AOL, as appealing as that might have been. CMGI also owned a profitable mail-order list and mutual fund literature fulfillment business, and it was reinvesting its profits—as well as the proceeds from its orderly sale of AOL stock—in a group of small, cutting-edge Internet companies.

What we, and later the market, found most alluring was the company's purchase of exclusive rights to Lycos spider technology. Developed at Carnegie-Mellon University, Lycos is a gargantuan online catalog that 35 million people per month use to search the Internet by subject. That makes it one of the most popular search engines on the Internet. To put those 35 million monthly searches in perspective, a much more famous and established search engine—*TV Guide*—has about 16 million subscribers.

CMGI stock did well before the Internet mania really started, but after the Netscape public offering it did much, much better, eventually rising from $4 to $50.25 in a year. The run-up was partly fueled by the company's announcement that it would spin off its Lycos, Inc. division to the public in 1996.

Due diligence had shown us that CMGI's top managers were adept at spotting great companies early—and buying substantial stakes at relatively low prices. The company's investments include a 38% stake in ProductView Interactive, a developer of advertiser-supported Internet products, and a 33% position in Ikonic Interactive, a developer of interactive multimedia.

In many ways, CMGI is like a publicly traded venture capital firm specializing in the Internet, arguably the fastest-growing business with the greatest potential in the world. That's why CMGI remains our favorite Internet position.

But that could change abruptly, even if the Internet continues its phenomenal growth. When a major theme remains in place, it always evolves in some way. Occasionally, that means yesterday's big winners become also-rans.

Look at the personal computer explosion. As PCs proliferated, local area network (LAN) companies became red-hot. The king of the hill, Novell, was a fantastic stock from the mid-1980s to 1992. Since then, Novell has fallen by about 65% during a powerful bull market. The main reason is that the recent torrid networking growth has been in wide area networks (WANS), dominated by Cisco Systems, Bay Networks, and Newbridge Networks, among others. And in the LAN business, Microsoft's NT has made serious inroads on Novell Netware's market share lead.

A Theme Within a Theme

Biotech companies will create many of the great new drugs of the future. That's a given, and it's a great theme. Some investors will undoubtedly profit from it. But others will lose their shirts. How can you tell, in early-stage trials, which drugs will be winners and which will be losers? It's difficult, and when you're wrong in biotech, you're really wrong. After a disappointment, a biotech stock can shed 90% of its value in a year. That's why biotech mutual funds can make so much sense.

Does that mean you should never touch a biotech stock? Not necessarily. If you find a company that meets an industry need but doesn't have all its chips riding on the success of a single specific drug, you may have an enormous winner. I think I've found one.

The company, Human Genome Sciences Inc. (HGSI), is the world leader in genomics technology. Among other things, it uses powerful computers and software to analyze the makeup of genes that cause specific diseases. HGSI then licenses this information to pharmaceutical companies. In exchange, it receives royalties if the pharmaceutical company develops successful drugs using HGSI's technology.

HGSI could be a great investment for several reasons:

- The world's eighth largest drug maker, Smithkline Beecham, has decided that genomics will revolutionize all drug development. It has signed a contract giving it exclusive access to all human genes analyzed by HGSI. (Nonhuman genes are a different story. HGSI can market those where it likes.)

  In 2001, all Smithkline Beecham patents gained through genomics revert to HGSI. That in itself is bullish on two fronts. If the patents are valuable, HGSI's stock should soar. And if it even looks as if the patents will have great value, Smithkline Beecham might simply buy out HGSI rather than lose the patents.

- The technology works. Smithkline Beecham announced in late 1995 that its osteoporosis drug candidate, developed with HGSI technology, looked extremely promising.

  In January 1996, HGSI made headlines by announcing that it had successfully analyzed more than 99% of the genetic structure of three of the most common in-hospital infections.

- In addition to leading to new drug discoveries, genomics is remarkably cost-effective. It can reduce the time it takes to discover a new drug by three years, thus saving a pharmaceutical company millions, or perhaps tens of millions, of dollars.

- HGSI's cost structure is lower than that of most biotech companies because it spends relatively little of its resources attempting to develop drugs of its own. This strategy minimizes the risk that it will be concentrating on the wrong drugs and will somehow burn through all its cash.

If HGSI realizes half of its potential, the upside could be enormous. But that doesn't mean it's a sure thing. In fact, there are those who have great doubts about the future of HGSI and Smithkline Beecham, and you need to know why. Never fall into the trap of looking at a theme in a vacuum. Always pay close attention to the downside risks.

The doubters note that Smithkline Beecham can only achieve spectacular results if it increases market share, which means that it will have to grow faster than other huge drug companies. But Smithkline has been a laggard in the past. You cannot back it without being aware that many on Wall Street think that Merck, the world's largest drugmaker—with a vaunted new-product delivery pipeline— will be able to withstand any challenge, no matter what kind of technology it's based on.

To go with HGSI, you have to believe that Merck will not win every battle it fights, that it is moving too slowly on the genome front (it has its own genome project but is thus far treating it gingerly), and that its traditional methods of achieving industry dominance may not work so well in the next decade. I'm willing to back these assumptions with my money, and I think that HGSI and Smithkline Beecham are better long-term investments than Merck.

If I think that both companies will prosper together, why do I own HGSI and not Smithkline Beecham? Because HGSI gives me more leverage. If I am right about the ultimate outcome, it will be the bigger winner.

THERAGENICS

One of the most compelling themes today involves new medical products or treatments that are more cost-efficient and less intrusive than existing methods. In today's climate, such innovations should receive enthusiastic reception, for three reasons:

1. Everyone in the health care system is under pressure to cut costs.

2. Consumers, who are paying for a growing share of their medical outlays, often demand that they receive the most cost-effective treatment.

3. Less intrusive procedures mean shorter hospital stays and fewer lost work days, both of which are desired by everyone involved in the health care loop.

Medical technology companies are now one of the leading groups in our hedge fund, accounting for about 35% of assets. One of those holdings, and a 1996 Magic 25 selection, is Theragenics.

Theragenics has a patented, FDA-approved treatment for prostate cancer, a procedure that boasts a 90% success rate. Its solution: to place radioactive palladium pellets—Theraseeds—inside the cancerous prostate.

Last year, about 150,000 men in the United States alone learned that they have prostate cancer. (Of late, that figure has been rising by 25% per year.) The procedures that compete with the Theragenics treatment are both highly undesirable. The first—removal of the prostate—often leads to impotence and incontinence. The second—external beam radiation—requires more than thirty visits to the doctor. It can cause impotence too, as well as painful urination and diarrhea.

A Theraseeds treatment has comparatively few side effects (impotence is one of them) and costs $10,000. A prostatectomy costs two to four times as much. Many hospitals prefer the Theragenics approach, but many surgeons opt to perform the more expensive surgical procedure.

The company is already profitable, and recent sales have been growing at a 70% rate. We recommended Theragenics at $6.13 and it rose as high as $18.63 in 1996. At last glance, it was trading at $16.88.

The Subtleties of a Trend

Some people take a big-picture approach that fails to address the nuances in an industry. Panicky sellers do this all the time. Sometimes, the market overreacts and trashes every stock in an industry indiscriminately, regardless of the individual stocks' prospects. This creates opportunities for a person who really knows the business.

A perfect example occurred from mid-1995 to early 1996. After a long rally, semiconductor stocks as a group sold off sharply. The largest ones—Intel, Texas Instruments, Micron Technology—were really clobbered. Some investors then concluded that if the industry was being hammered, it must be time to sell all chip stocks, especially the smaller ones that might not withstand a downturn so well.

That logic was terribly flawed. Investors were unloading the leading chipmakers because their pricing power was being eroded. But some niche chipmakers weren't facing any new competition and still had a great deal of pricing power. So, even as Micron lost half of its value, Oak Technologies, a great company in an entirely different segment of the chip business, was more than doubling in price.

The same rules apply to buying a business and picking a stock. Both activities will yield better results when you have the wind at your back—when you're investing in a strong part of the economy that is likely to get much stronger.

7

Staying on Top

One vital investment technique I use is different in kind from all the others, although it's no less valuable. I call it "updates:" keeping an eye out for important developments in a select group of stocks.

Relying heavily on updates can improve your investing discipline. In part, this is because it forces you to address the essential question so many investors ignore: Knowing what I now know, would I buy this stock today? There's no need to drive yourself crazy by reevaluating the prospects of all your stocks on an hourly basis, but frequent reassessment is vital.

At least once a month, you should perform a buy, sell, or hold analysis—however rudimentary—on all your holdings. Revisiting your portfolio isn't an intellectual parlor game. If one of your stocks still looks like a screaming buy, seriously consider buying more. If you conclude it's a sell, then sell. If it's a hold, ask, "Can I replace it with something better?"

Although being chronically impatient is not an investing virtue, most individuals inhabit the other end of the investing spectrum. They hold stocks much longer than they should. It's important to understand the reasons.

- Taking a loss means acknowledging a mistake (sometimes, a lulu). Humans don't like admitting mistakes. Everyone would prefer not to have to 'fess up. Trouble is, time may heal all wounds, but it doesn't eventually levitate all securities.

- People get emotionally involved with their stocks. Often, they fall in love. Or they concentrate on the stock's virtues and minimize its flaws. Their investment in the company isn't purely financial. They care. They become reluctant to let go.

- Stockholders fear that as soon as they sell, trumpets will sound and the good news about the company will finally be proclaimed throughout the land. Yes, this could happen. In fact, if you invest frequently enough, I promise you that it *will* happen. I screw up this way at least several times a year, year after year.

  Nonetheless, over time, such portfolio adjustments will dramatically improve your investment returns. There are several lessons here, but the wrong message reads: Never sell, something good might happen.

- Selling stock A to buy stock B looks expensive. You're right; it ain't cheap. Commissions can eat you alive if you trade too much. But the phrase "penny wise, pound foolish" does come to mind. Does it make any sense to hold onto a clunker because you don't want to incur another buy/sell commission? Is the avoidance of transaction costs your number-one investment goal?

  In most cases, a 2%, 3%, or 5% return differential will cover the extra commissions. That's not an enormous amount of money. To "save" the 5% and avoid switching into a stock that goes up 50%, 100%, or 200% is not my idea of a shrewd bargain.

GETTING OUT ALIVE

Besides making you a lot of money, a sound update mechanism can save you a fortune. As an example, consider Jennifer Convertibles, not one of my finest picks by a long shot. Jennifer was a mistake. A big one. But a timely update kept it from becoming a disaster.

Actually, Jennifer was two mistakes. The nation's largest sofabed retailer was a *Special Situations Report* (SSR) selection in February 1993 at $13.75. Almost a year later, we compounded our error by making Jennifer a 1994 Magic 25 selection at the identical price. It wouldn't be $13.75 for long.

We liked the fact that Paramus, New Jersey-based Jennifer (market cap, $78.4 million) had adopted an expansion strategy of adding new stores via licensing rather than owning them outright. We considered this a low-risk, low-capital method of expanding.

The new strategy wasn't hurting earnings. In its recently concluded fiscal year, Jennifer's earnings rose 50% to $0.51 per share. Revenues rose only 19%, but that was because of the licensing emphasis (at licensed stores, only royalties, as opposed to sales, were booked as revenues).

We changed our view of the company when we read the press release detailing information on May sales. The release was a nightmare. First, the news was dreadful. Worse yet, the company wasn't candid. (Besides supporting the value of updates, the Jennifer story is also a cautionary tale about what to pay attention to and what to ignore in a company press release.)

The least relevant piece of information was the fact that the combined gain in revenues from company-owned and licensed stores was 40% in May. Sounds great, but it didn't factor in the addition of new stores. The numbers that deserved close scrutiny were the increase in revenues at company-owned stores and the increase in royalty income from licensed stores.

Did I say increase? There wasn't one. Same-store sales were down 11% from March, a comparison even more atrocious than it seems because during March 1995 the weather in the Northeast—Jennifer's primary marketing area—was horrible. How did May 1995 sales compare to May 1994 sales? Inexcusably, Jennifer chose not to compute the figure. (Must be because the news was so good, right?)

Royalty income grew only 9%, another major disappointment. Jennifer also reported that it had stopped accepting royalties from LP2, a partnership that had funded 20 licensed stores in the Midwest.

Furthermore, the company reported that the net profit margin at company-owned stores, once 5.5%, had fallen to about 2.4% because of the expense of opening and operating the new line of Jennifer Leather stores. After crunching some numbers, we concluded that there was no way that Jennifer was going to meet our $0.60 earnings target for the fiscal year that would end in three months. In fact, there was now a good chance that its earnings wouldn't exceed, or might not even match, last year's $0.51 per share.

Our conclusions: Profit growth had stalled, the expansion strategy was in trouble, and Jennifer's management had just shown a disturbing willingness to try to shield investors from the hard facts. We decided to vote with our feet, telling SSR subscribers in July to dump Jennifer at $8.75 and advising *Individual Investor* readers to do likewise at the same price in August. The result of our Jennifer experience: a humbling loss of 36%.

After we sold, the news got much worse. The next quarter, Jennifer reported earnings of $0.15. Fine on the surface, but the company noted that more than half of net income—$0.08—came from an accounting change. Without the change, the earnings were lousy. (For the second month in a row, Jennifer opted not to publish same-store sales comparisons. This oversight was becoming habitual. We might have forgiven the company for doing this once, but not twice. As Voltaire said about patronizing a brothel: "Once, a philosopher. Twice, a pervert.")

The market responded by hammering the stock down by nearly 50%. Still, this marked another possible exit point for the alert investor.

Earnings continued soft—and then a major scandal erupted. It turned out that managers had set up a separate company, which they owned, to sell furniture to Jennifer. At best, this was an unconscionable conflict of interest. (The executives had an incentive to overcharge Jennifer for product. Their small company could make money even if Jennifer's profits declined or disappeared.) At worst, the arrangement was outright fraud. The SEC began investigating.

Then Jennifer failed to file its quarterly financial statements (the excuse—sometimes valid, but usually not—was that results were delayed because of a change in accounting methods). Next, the company projected a big loss and its general counsel resigned. On April 17, 1995, the stock was de-listed by NASDAQ. That day, the market converted Jennifer into a stock selling for $1.75.

A month later, Jennifer's auditors withdrew their opinion on the company's 1993 annual report.

THE POWER OF THE TECHNIQUE

- The update approach works so often because it relies on an irrefutable investing principle: The more you know about a company, the more likely you'll make the correct investment decision. When you update, you gain new information and perspective.

- Relying on updates helps weed out the losers and laggards. If your followup brings forth nothing but bad news, something is probably wrong—no, something is almost *definitely* wrong. Unless you have a great reason for believing that circumstances will soon change, or unless you think that the stock has been beaten down so much that it is now trading for less than its liquidation value, I'd consider selling.

BEING RIGHT TWICE

Nonetheless, companies do change. We've been right about McAfee Associates twice, for example—but for entirely different reasons.

We chose McAfee as a 1994 Magic 25 selection because, having been beaten down to $6.25 (market cap, $70 million), it had become a value play. The Santa Clara, California-based world leader in antivirus software was no longer growing fast, but it had a low P/E ratio, fat profit margins, and a lot of cash on hand.

McAfee's performance was pretty magical. After a year, the stock had gained 124%, reaching $14 (market cap, $170.8 million). But what should we do now? We concluded that it was not time to take profits. In fact, after a careful reexamination of the company, we decided that McAfee was not the same company we had recommended twelve months before. It was better.

When we first recommended it, McAfee was a high-margin, one-product company with lots of cash and relatively slow earnings growth. Its new CEO said he wanted to expand McAfee's software offerings.

But almost everyone in corporate America talks a good game. Part of the update strategy is to recognize early when a CEO starts *delivering* on those tantalizing promises. McAfee CEO Bill Larsen was delivering. Larsen had used acquisitions and internal product development to transform McAfee into a network management software powerhouse. Better still, Larsen was taking one of the company's great strengths and leveraging it to the hilt.

Another reason we first liked McAfee: It is a truly innovative, twenty-first-century company. It has almost no sales infrastructure. Instead, it sells its software via commercial online services and on the Internet. A user who wants the software downloads it and then pays McAfee.

Does everybody pay? No, but the deadbeat ratio is lower than you might think. That's because most of McAfee's customers are large corporations. And the company is even philosophical about its nonpaying customers. It knows a lot of cyberpunks steal the software, but many of them end up recommending it to paying customers. The CEO called the process "sampling."

Of those who do pay, most work in corporate MIS departments. McAfee already has an 80% penetration of the Fortune 100 market for its antivirus software, which makes it much easier for the company to sell new software to the same people.

As it came time to draw up the 1995 Magic 25 list, we were faced with a fairly common, but not altogether unpleasant, stockholder dilemma. What do you do with a stock that has more than doubled in less than a year? Sell? Hold? Buy more?

Here's why we decided to buy more.

Granted, McAfee was no longer dirt cheap as a value stock, but that wasn't why we liked it so much. It was once again a growth stock. As an added benefit, it was becoming a major player in one of the fastest-growing markets around.

Even though the stock had doubled, the market had yet to fully recognize the new, transformed McAfee. The stock was selling at just 15 times our 1995 earnings estimate—a below-market multiple and a valuation 50% lower than that of comparable software companies.

If you read Chapter 1, you know the happy outcome. Four months later, McAfee hit $31, a gain of another 121%. The total return for sixteen months: 396%.

The key point here is that McAfee had become a different company than it was when we first recommended it, and we were rewarded for noticing. Had it remained a slow-growing, cash-rich enterprise, we probably would have had no right to expect more than a double.

Interestingly, when we have selected a company for the Magic 25 for a second time, it has usually done very well. Although the sample size is fairly small, it is safe to say that the success rate is attributable to the update function. By the time we chose the company as a repeat selection, we knew a tremendous amount about it. We had an edge. And we capitalized on it.

Sometimes, we wait years before recommending a former favorite again. Consider Mylex Corporation, a Fremont, California, technology company that had appeared on our very first Magic 25 list in 1992. That year, we considered it a turnaround play and it gained 60%. But it never made the bottom-line progress we expected, so we said *so long*, but not *goodbye*. As usual, we kept watching the company.

Three years later, in 1995, the same managers, whom we respected, had changed almost everything about Mylex. The company, which had once specialized in computer motherboards, had recreated itself as a leader in the "disk array controller" market. Mylex is a leader in redundant array of independent disks (RAID) technology. Essentially, RAID helps customers achieve the safety level of huge mainframes without the enormous cost. Mylex's customers, such as IBM and Digital Equipment, incorporate its technology into their own computers. Translation: When PC-based computer networks crash, Mylex products prevent companies from losing crucial data.

As 1995 began, Mylex owned one half of the $133-million board-level disk array industry, a segment that was expected to nearly double by 1996. At the new Mylex, disk array products accounted for 80% of sales. At a price of $8.88 (market cap, $131.3 million), we rated Mylex a repeat buy.

Mylex turned profitable once again, reporting quarterly earnings in the first quarter of 1995. Gradually, the market recognized that Mylex had indeed undergone an extraordinary transformation. By May 1995, the stock hit $12.63, a gain of 42.5% in five months.

The Mylex we liked in 1995 was almost unrecognizable from the Mylex we backed in 1992. And there's absolutely nothing wrong with that. Above all, an update system makes it clear that yesterday's winner could be tomorrow's loser or laggard—or a 500% gainer. How the story pans out depends on many different variables, most of which you can analyze as the months and years pass.

Do You Update Forever?

The idea that we waited three years before repurchasing Mylex might unnerve some investors. You might wonder: Should my watch list include every stock I've ever owned or contemplated buying? Of course not. When you sell, you're not committed to following your discarded merchandise for a lifetime, no matter what.

But if you have owned a stock, you *are* in a better position to apply the update method. Don't feel burdened by the expectation that you have to track every security you've ever known, but be aware that there are cumulative advantages to updating stocks you know. Over time, you'll have a better sense of when to get in and when to get out.

WHERE TO GET THE INFORMATION

In one sense, people interested in the stock market are always updating, whether consciously or not. They do this simply by paying attention to what they read and see in the world.

When you read your daily paper, *The Wall Street Journal,* business publications, or trade journals, be especially alert for items that concern stocks in your portfolio and on your watch list. Many publications, including the *Journal, The New York Times, Forbes, Fortune,* and Individual Investor, simplify updating by including an index of company listings in every issue.

Pay attention as well to industry overview pieces relating to companies you follow. Although a story on network management software may not mention McAfee or PC DOCS directly, I still read every word.

If you're in touch with people at the company, this kind of big-picture article can prompt intelligent questions. "What are you doing about a certain segment of the market? How directly do you compete with company X? Where do you have an advantage? Where do competitors lead? What are you planning to do about it?"

Here are some additional tips for keeping up with companies:

- Go directly to the source. Call the investor relations department and ask to be put on the mailing list for press releases, quarterly reports, annual reports, and so on. Almost every company will do this for you if you sound serious. If you get a tepid response initially, make it clear that you're thinking of becoming a shareholder.

- Subscribe to an online service. Many services offer brief summaries of every news item about a company during the recent past (the time period is often a year or longer). That might be overkill, but if you're just starting to follow a company, a quick scan of the headlines could help get you up to speed quickly.

- Cultivate any contacts you have with Wall Street analysts. Ask whether they're still neutral on stock Z. Get a clear sense of what circumstances might transform that neutral rating into a buy.

A Strategy

With stocks on your watch list, it pays to think of the old baseball expression, "Wait for your pitch." Translation: There's no rush to buy. You'll do best if you wait until conditions at a company change in a manner that is truly likely to affect its share price.

An important corollary: Sometimes, the trigger event you want to see never occurs. You won't end up buying every stock on your watch list. When the pitcher tosses every ball in the dirt, you don't have to swing.

Example: I've been waiting more than two years for Micro Healthsystems to become a winner. My guess is that success is at least six months away, if not longer.

In short, Micro Healthsystems has a good product. Its bedside computers are designed to monitor a hospital patient's condition and manage patient risk. They work just fine. They can actually save money over time, but amid the *sturm und drang* of the Clintonian health care debate and the industry's cost-cutting frenzy, the logical customers didn't come through with their expected orders. My money was in the wrong place at the wrong time. The New Jersey-based company was an SSR selection in August 1992 at a price of $17. Now it's $3.38.

At this point, I'm not sure Micro Healthsystems will ever be a success. But I can say two good things about the company: (1) its technology is fine, and (2) its management, which holds a substantial ownership stake, seems honest and straightforward.

But those aren't sufficient reasons to buy the stock. I'm avoiding it now because management says the next two or three quarters will continue to be unprofitable.

What am I waiting for? Comments by the company indicating that profitability is just a quarter away. Or, news of a huge new contract that will pretty much guarantee a profitable quarter. Or, a powerful burst of insider buying.

If none of these events occurs, Micro Healthsystems may remain on my watch list, but I won't be buying any shares. That's right. Even though I can pick up the shares for 80% less than I paid three years ago, I don't consider them a bargain, because the company's promise hasn't panned out. And maybe it never will.

Sometimes you know what event to expect—or hope for—and sometimes you don't have a clue. I made a quick killing on Pharmhouse in 1995, on news that came out of left field.

Pharmhouse Corporation, based in New York, is the owner of a small chain of deep-discount drugstores. In 1994, Pharmhouse stock fluctuated between $0.38 and $1.25. Its market cap ranged from $836,000 to $2.8 million. Even at a paltry valuation of $836,000, I chose not to nibble. I knew something could propel the shares higher, but I didn't know what it would be.

In 1995, Pharmhouse announced that it had signed an agreement to acquire Woolworth's 24-store deep-discount drug chain. This was an immense deal for a company that, at the moment, had only 14 stores.

My immediate thinking went like this: First, this was one of those wonderful occasions when a huge American institution unloads a small, no-longer-relevant portion of its empire to an opportunistic small-cap upstart. Second, there were many reasons to believe that the purchase would allow Pharmhouse to benefit from new economies of scale.

To my astonishment, the stock didn't move on the news. I was able to buy shares at $0.94, the pre-announcement price.

On Monday, the stock opened unchanged. Then it began making up for lost time. By Tuesday, it had hit $1.75. By Wednesday, it got as high as $2.88. Within two weeks, it reached $4.38. That's a gain of 366% in half a month. On an annualized basis, that's a return so large my calculator might explode if I tried to figure it out.

Was this an overnight investment success? Yes and no. After all, I had been following the company closely for two years. I was waiting for the right moment, the key update, to come along. When it did, I pounced.

Other Successes

A company that couldn't be in a more different business than McAfee was an update success for a very similar reason. It, too, had a better way of distributing a bigger line of products.

Duluth, Georgia-based AGCO Corporation proves that a well-run company with a better idea can achieve great results, no matter what industry it's in. AGCO makes and distributes heavy farm equipment. For a long time, AGCO was a relatively small player in the farm equipment business. Three years ago, CEO Robert Ratliff hit on a new strategy designed to transform the company. Realizing that AGCO wasn't operating in one of the world's great growth markets, Ratliff decided to gain market share and increase profits by broadening the product mix at the company's dealerships. AGCO would accomplish this by acquiring some manufacturing companies, as well as distribution rights to other brands.

The goal: To have AGCO dealers offer the broadest product line in the industry. The approach seemed entirely reasonable to us, and we put AGCO on our watch list.

Earnings reports indicated that the new marketing strategy was working. In the second quarter of 1993, AGCO earned $0.93 versus $0.02 the previous year. We decided to recommend the stock in September 1993 at $13.

In the third quarter, AGCO again reported stunning results, with earnings of $1.07 versus $0.26. AGCO was competing more effectively with industry leader John Deere than it ever had before. Although the stock had risen to $18, we wrote an update stating that AGCO was still a buy.

Fabulous earnings continued quarter after quarter (with gains of 600%, 49%, 34%, 163%, and 98%). In April 1994, AGCO announced that it was buying the entire Massey Ferguson unit from Varity Corp. By May 1995, AGCO was trading at $39.88, a gain of 122% in the 18 months since our update and 207% in the 21 months following our original recommendation. And its P/E ratio was still only 6. We never expected AGCO to be a high-multiple stock, but we believed there was some room for multiple expansion.

SPOTTING TURNAROUNDS

The update mechanism often allows you to spot turnaround situations early. Minneapolis-based Zeos International, for example, used to be one the nation's leading mail-order PC vendors. In 1992, the company lost its touch. From 1992 until mid-1994, it didn't post a single profitable quarter. From a high above $20, Zeos stock plunged to below $3 a share. We reported on the company in November 1992 and really weren't convinced that the story would have a happy ending. (Our title: "Phoenix or Cadaver?")

In November 1994, however, we revisited the company and wrote a bullish update. What had changed? Zeos the laggard had introduced some appealing new products, such as the Meridian 800C color notebook computer and the Pantera line of desktop systems. The products were actually selling. In the second quarter of 1994, sales increased 46% and Zeos returned to profitability, earning $0.06 per share.

Given the positive sales and earnings trend, and the fact that the company had $12.9 million in cash, we decided that Zeos was a buy at $3.

It sure was. Earnings surprised everyone who cared about Zeos, and the stock quickly doubled. It was trading at $9 when a larger rival made a bid to acquire Zeos. The stock ceased trading at $12 in April 1995, giving our readers a 300% gain in five months.

Here's another story of how updates can offer a second chance. In September 1990, First Team Sports became one of our first SSR selections at a price of $7.25. We liked the company because it had a strong position in the low end of the in-line skates market. We thought in-line skating would continue to experience phenomenal growth.

We were right about the market but wrong about the stock. First Team Sports, headquartered in Mounds View, Minnesota, never seemed to find a way to make money consistently in this great growth business. So, three years and one month after our SSR recommendation, we sold the stock for $7.25, our purchase price. Talk about dead money.

But we kept tracking the company. Before long, we noticed that things were changing. For the quarter ended May 1, 1994, the company posted record sales and earnings. Net income rose 188% to $0.29 per share, and gross margins doubled to 29%.

In addition, First Team Sports announced that the year's six-month revenues would probably exceed total 1993 sales. The reason: rapidly growing orders of low-end in-line skates (average price, $70) by Wal-Mart and Kmart. It was time to update our opinion.

Although the in-line skates market was still booming (there were 34% more skaters in 1993 than in 1992), we knew that kind of growth couldn't possibly be sustained. So we wanted to know what First Team Sports was planning for an encore. The answer was an increased emphasis on street hockey equipment, which currently contributed 10% to revenues.

But, given the company's rapid growth—and with analysts projecting 1995 fiscal year earnings of $0.67 a share—we thought the stock was cheap at a split-adjusted price of $8.83. So we recommended it in November 1994.

In January 1995, First Team Sports announced spectacular earnings. Sales more than doubled to $24.3 million, and earnings rose 240% to $0.34 per share.

A week later, the company declared a three-for-two stock split. In April, it again came in with blockbuster earnings. By mid-1995, First Team Sports was trading at $26, a gain of 194% since we had taken a second look at the company.

Because my specialty is small-cap investing, some people assume that I automatically look fondly on any tiny company that might have a big future. That's ridiculous.

Consider Iwerks Entertainment, based in Burbank, California, one of the world leaders in virtual reality technology. Virtual reality may be the entertainment medium of the future. But in April 1994, *Individual Investor*, mincing words as usual, called Iwerks "a stupidly overpriced stock" at $24.25, even though it had recently been as high as $37.

Just two months later, the stock was down to $11. Sometimes, this kind of free fall presents investors with a buying opportunity. We decided to analyze Iwerks again.

No buying opportunity here. To begin with, Iwerks was still trading at 100 times the most bullish analyst's earnings projections for 1995. And, because of the decline in its stock, Iwerks would now have to shell out an additional 175,000 shares to acquire Omni Films International, a money-losing film company. We concluded that Iwerks was still expensive at $11. Within a year, shares were changing hands at $3.50.

What went wrong? Plenty. In fact, nothing seemed to go right. When a company is trading at 100 or 200 times projected earnings, a lot of things have to go right.

In October, three of the company's five outside directors resigned—a bad sign. Later that month, Iwerks laid off 13% of its workforce. In February 1995, it let go another 10%. And, almost needless to say, none of those projected earnings came through.

SPECIAL SITUATIONS

Updates are always potentially valuable, but they can be particularly important in certain investment situations.

Biotech or Other "Concept" Companies

I've had some big winners and some cataclysmic losers in biotech, but I've learned from some of my mistakes. I now think updates are the best way to play biotech.

The big biotech and medical device winners (Amgen, Chiron, and so on) usually begin sustainable, long-term upward moves for one of three reasons: (1) the FDA approves a drug or device with huge potential; (2) a drug or device proves to be a hit with the medical community; or (3) the company reports that profits (yes, these companies are actually supposed to make money at some point) exceed analyst expectations.

What is the main reason individual investors often do so badly in biotech? They overpay for a risky security. The mistake is entirely understandable. Human nature guides people to a specific biotech company after a promising product receives favorable publicity. However, by the time that happens, hype has already worked its magic on the stock price. In almost every case, this is the *wrong* time to buy. You can bet that the stock price is 50% too high and that there will almost certainly be a better buying opportunity later.

Consider what happened when Cetus announced that its Interleukin 2 was successful in curing some inoperable cancers. Can you imagine a company reporting better good news? Cetus had closed at $33 the day before the announcement. The next day, it traded at $40—in the morning.

After that, it was all downhill.

Six months later, Cetus was at $18. What happened? The company's cancer cure announcement was legit, as far as it went.

Unfortunately for those arriving late to the party, most people in the medical/biotech community suspected that Interleukin 2 was effective. They bid up the stock in anticipation of the good news. Too much hype had worked its predictable effects on the stock price.

The lesson is: When you buy a biotech company, either purchase it for a price close to the amount of cash the company has per share, or conclude that the news you're buying on is truly monumental and has definite long-term significance.

A wonderful example is Thermo Cardiosystems of Waltham, Massachusetts, developers of the revolutionary heart pump (technically, a left ventricular-assist device, or LVAD) that can keep people alive—and fully ambulatory—while they're waiting for a replacement heart. The company had to wait years before the pump was finally approved by the FDA.

During that seemingly endless waiting period, many Americans who needed heart transplants died. They were the real casualties of the delay, but shareholders suffered as well. They had every reason to think that the company had made a good product, but, without marketing approval, the stock simply languished.

Personally, I got tired of waiting. My money wasn't exactly dead, but it did seem to be on life support. I had made only a 27% profit in my seventeen months of ownership of Thermo Cardiosystems' parent, Thermedics.

I waited long enough to see FDA approval announced, but I got frustrated and sold too soon. I missed the real action.

After the FDA gave its blessing, more good news followed. On March 22, 1995, major insurance companies said that they would reimburse patients who used the pump. Earnings rose sharply, quintupling in the quarter announced May 8, 1995. Thermo Cardiosystems went on an upward romp. From $15 on December 2, 1994, it jumped to $37.63 on May 15, 1995, a gain of 151%.

There are two lessons here. First, in most cases, formal marketing approval is a major positive development for a small company. The exception occurs when there has been so much hype that the shares are already priced upward in a happy response to the approval process.

Second, the update process could have made you money weeks or months *after* FDA approval of the heart pump, whether you had bailed out of the stock early (as I did) or had just kept it on your watch list. Remember: you could have paid $15 for Thermo Cardio-systems after FDA approval.

The best investors use updates to correct their mistakes. Updates offer a second chance.

Here's another example of how you can turn an investing mistake into a major success. We first wrote about Interneuron Pharmaceuticals in our February 1994 biotech issue. The promising Lexington, Massachusetts, company was trading at $9 at the time, giving it a market cap of $258 million. By the end of the year, the price had been nearly cut in half, to $5.

We could have cursed our luck (well, we did a little) and abandoned the stock, but we saw absolutely no deterioration in Interneuron's fundamentals. In fact, as the stock sagged, insider buying perked up. Major purchases were made in May, June, July, August, and October.

And the company was now trading at a price suggesting that its most promising drug had no chance of FDA approval. Not only did we disagree with that assessment, but we felt that the pickup in insider buying suggested that those closest to the situation disagreed as well.

Interneuron's most promising drug is easier to understand than it is to pronounce. Dexfenfluramine—Dex, for short—is taken orally and stimulates the release of serotonin in the brain. The release of serotonin, the same chemical released by the ingestion of carbohydrates and fats, tricks the brain into thinking that the body's hunger has been satiated.

If all this sounds somewhat familiar, the action of Dex is similar to that of Prozac. Eli Lilly, Prozac's developer, considered marketing Prozac as an obesity drug at one point. One problem: Unlike Dex, Prozac requires ever-greater doses to help patients keep weight off.

One of the best things about Dex is that, unlike some other promising drugs, it is already known that Dex works on actual people. Ten million customers in Europe swear by it, and the drug has proven to be effective in human trials. The potential market is mouthwatering: Americans spent more than $10 billion on diet products in 1994 alone.

As we updated Interneuron's progress, we noted that its other drugs were coming along nicely. They include Citicoline, a treatment for stroke and head trauma (if the drug wins FDA approval in 1997, it could contribute more to Interneuron's bottom line than Dex); Bucindolol, a cardiovascular drug slated to enter Phase III trials in 1995; an antianxiety drug; a treatment for Parkinson's disease; a circadian rhythm regulator; and, of all things, a high-powered sports drink.

All told, Interneuron had seven drugs in development and five in advanced clinical trials. Yes, the stock would suffer if the FDA delayed or denied approval for Dex. But there were more than enough reasons to like the stock without Dex.

At the bargain price of $5, we made Interneuron a 1995 Magic 25 selection. Then the news started to develop nicely. A month later, chairman Morton Davis bought 5,000 additional shares. In March 1995, the FDA announced that it might ease the rules for diet drug approval. After the FDA announcement, one thing was clear: The agency was putting diet drugs on the fast track for approval. The next month, Interneuron learned that its Bucindolol had become the only heart drug to be approved for use in Phase III trials by the National Institutes of Health.

By May 1, 1995, Interneuron had reached $8.88, an increase of 78% in about five months.

GOING BACK FOR MORE

If you think it's hard to sell at loss, it's probably even harder to get back into a stock at a price higher than when you sold. I know some otherwise intelligent investors who just cannot bring themselves to do it—ever.

Why is it so difficult?

- It opens up an old wound.

- A stock that has soared since you sold it is no longer a friend. If you sold Microsoft at $10 and watched it rise to $85, you've been rooting against the company for years. You want to see the Justice Department break it up. You want to see Bill Gates indicted. You want the company's new program to have more bugs than your backyard.

  It's hard to buy shares in a company you've learned to hate.

- You don't want to screw up again. You worry that the stock might tank as soon as you buy it.

The reasons all make sense, but it would be wonderful if you could overcome them. The company doesn't know that you were ever a shareholder. It's not thinking of ways to trip you up or cause you grief.

If the company has changed significantly since you sold, that doesn't make you an idiot. Try to look at the stock's prospects with fresh eyes. Is the stock going up for the right reasons? Is there much upside potential left?

Remember: Having previously owned the company gives you an advantage. You know the business better than most investors. You know the potential problems. I try to profit from every edge I can get. Don't ignore yours. Here's what can happen when you do.

I know someone who discovered Micron Technology way before I did. Joe bought the stock for $1.38 in 1986. Pretty smart. He sold a year later at $2, making a nifty profit of 45%.

Micron's business began to improve. (We recommended the stock at $5 in 1992.) But the higher Micron went, the more upset Joe got. He wouldn't buy Micron at $5 because it was already 150% higher than his sale price. And he wouldn't buy it at $10. How could he touch a stock that had quintupled since he unloaded it?

And, according to his logic, if he wouldn't buy at $5 or $10, he certainly wasn't going to buy at $20. Or $30. Or $50. Or $67.75. Or $88.50, the price Micron reached in May 1995.

In Joe's defense, very few people could jump back in after leaving a 1,000% or 2,000% profit on the table. But huge changes had taken place in the chip business since the late 1980s. The need for chips was growing enormously, and the threat from Japanese semiconductor companies no longer loomed as large. The sharp rise in the yen versus the dollar and the growing technological leadership of American companies had totally altered the competitive landscape.

An investor can only see such things if he or she is actually looking. If the very mention of Micron, however, causes nothing but pain, you can't really be looking. You're just suffering and, perhaps even worse, you're neglecting an opportunity for enormous profits.

Try reframing the situation. Instead of thinking that selling at $2 and buying at $8 marks you as a fool, look at it this way. Buying at $8 is what the great investors do. It's a sign of character, an indication of clear thinking and objectivity. All that matters today is whether the stock is a buy at $8 or not. Where it used to trade is irrelevant.

Remember one thing: Don't dive back in merely because you can't stand the pain anymore. That's not an objective decision. It's an emotional one—and giving in to emotions is one of the worst things an investor can do.

A similar emotional problem can arise even if you never owned the stock. Let's say stock X has been on your watch list. You've watched it go up, but haven't done anything about it. Investors commonly succumb to their feelings in this situation. They decide not to buy because the stock is 20%, 40%, or 102% higher than when they first spotted it. Or, after sitting on the sidelines while the stock had a spectacular run, they plunge in—no matter what the price—because simply watching the stock has become too uncomfortable. They just have to participate.

If either of these approaches succeeds, it will be for the wrong reasons. Between the emotional extremes of "I can't buy it" and "No,

I must buy it," there isn't much to choose. Long term, they'll both lead to misfortune.

To turn this chapter on its head for a moment: Can you imagine becoming an outstanding investor without finding an effective update methodology? It can't be done.

The key issue, though, is how you integrate this approach into your investing life. Updating should be a consistent, but not obsessive, pursuit. Yes, things change. But material change doesn't occur every twelve seconds.

Stay in touch with the companies you own and those you're thinking of buying. In both cases, have a sense of what events might change your view of a company.

And if your view does change, act quickly and with confidence. Updates won't always work, but they'll make you money—and save you money—most of the time.

8

Mutual Funds

MANAGING THE MANAGERS

Everyone in America, it seems, loves mutual funds. Except me.

Let me explain. Mutual funds can be undeniably wonderful investments for millions of people. Some investors should probably own nothing but mutual funds. If you have taken the time to read this book, however, you are probably not one of them.

My main objection to mutual funds is simple. People who invest in them heavily will hardly ever achieve the spectacular returns talented stock investors can realize. The greater the percentage of your money that you have in mutual funds, the lower the chances that you'll beat the market averages.

Over a ten-year period, for instance, no fund has ever delivered a 30% annual return. Stretch the time frame out some more, and hardly any fund will have a prayer of returning 20% a year.

What about the legendary Magellan Fund? When it was managed by Peter Lynch, the fund had an average annual return of about 29.2%. For a mutual fund, that is astonishing. No other fund was even close.

The terrific performance of Magellan and a few other stellar funds obscures a more sobering truth about the entire mutual fund universe. After deducting all fees and expenses, the average mutual fund actually underperforms the market averages. In any given year, two out of every three funds will produce a return that is worse than the Standard & Poor's 500 index. With those odds, it is a trying task indeed to identify the handful of managers who have the potential to beat the market.

That's why I avoid mutual funds. But that doesn't necessarily mean that you should steer clear of them in every case, or that, when you choose a fund, you should have to settle for one that underperforms the averages.

GOOD REASONS TO USE MUTUAL FUNDS

Provided you don't overdo your stake in them, funds are a great tool for diversification and safety. They often make sense for people who don't want all their stock holdings to be in more volatile companies. If you feel this way, a logical response is to construct a portfolio that contains some individual stocks, as well as a core holding of mutual funds.

You don't have to swing for the fences with all your money. One reason funds are ultimately more conservative is that they offer investors a significant amount of diversification. Diversification diminishes an investor's risk by spreading assets among a much larger group of stocks. The typical equity mutual fund owns about 100 stocks. (Magellan owns approximately 400.) This greatly limits your downside risk.

I'm a believer in diversification—but only up to a point. Diversification provides investors with a kind of insurance policy. It's fine to buy such a policy, as long as you realize that it can be expensive. Owning hundreds of stocks almost invariably limits your potential for profit.

Bond mutual funds are also logical holdings for an investor who values income and stability above capital appreciation. A warning here, however. As many investors discovered to their horror in 1994—when rising interest rates caused the bond market to suffer its worst year since the Great Depression—bond funds aren't always stable, nor do they offer a guaranteed way to preserve capital.

Before you buy a bond fund, consider purchasing high-quality individual government or corporate bonds instead. If you are looking for a guaranteed return, only the U.S. government can provide that. Top-rated corporate or municipal bonds come in a close second.

Turbo-Charged Mutual Fund Strategies

In addition to these relatively conservative uses of mutual funds, there are also more strategic—and more aggressive—ways to deploy them. In Chapter 6, we discussed how to identify and profit from big economic trends. Sometimes, buying a fund may be the best way to play a specific sector or trend.

Let's say that, in 1991, you decided that the future of biotech not only looked bright—it has always *looked* extraordinary—but many companies in the industry were finally going to start generating profits. Had you tried the stock-picking approach, you might have been smart enough to buy Amgen at a split-adjusted price of $7. Two years later, it hit $78.

Then again, you might have chosen Xoma. It traded at $30 as recently as 1992. Three years later, you could buy it for $1.50. But Xoma did much better than Greenwich Pharmaceuticals. Greenwich hit $15 in 1992. In 1996, it traded for about 28 cents.

Granted, you could unearth similar examples of triumph and calamity in any industry. But, I have found that biotechnology is one of the most difficult sectors for the individual investor—and even the average investment professional—to figure out. If you're trying to pick out specific winners and losers, it is not enough to realize that the industry's overall potential is vast.

Biotech stocks are simply hard for an outsider to analyze. There may be no sales to track, for example. And that means there are no customers to interview. In most cases, there probably won't be any earnings.

In addition, a host of other things that are impossible for a non-expert to predict may derail a particular company's stock. A bally-hooed product may not work. It may work but still not get FDA approval. It may be superseded by a competing product that works better and has fewer side effects.

That's why I think it makes sense to rely on the judgment of a fund manager who is a biotech expert. There are benefits to entrusting your money to someone who understands the science involved, the competition, and the complicated FDA approval process. In biotech—more than in any other field—a piece of disappointing news can lead to the extinction of a company.

Funds can help you profit from other significant trends besides biotech. Take computer networking. For years, many investors have avoided networking stocks because they have looked expensive, as terrific stocks often do. Although we recommended Stratacom when it was trading at 100 times earnings, I can understand why any reader might say, "I don't chase stocks with three-figure P/Es."

That's where mutual funds might come in. They can lessen the risk, and the discomfort, of pursuing such high fliers.

But, you say, there's no mutual fund that specializes in computer networking. In the narrow sense, that's certainly true. But even though there is no networking fund per se, it is easy to find out which technology funds have particularly large stakes in the field. Instead of buying Stratacom, Cisco Systems, Bay Networks, or Newbridge Networks, you can buy a fund that has significant holdings in all of them.

Choosing a sector fund may also be appropriate if you are worried that you're a bit late for the party. One good recent example is semiconductor companies. As I mentioned in Chapter 6, chip stocks had a phenomenal run from 1992 to the end of 1994. Let's say that, as 1995 dawned, you liked the group but wanted to avoid the risk of losing 40% to 60% in any one stock. Instead of buying high-flying Micron Technology, you could have bought the Fidelity Select Electronics Fund instead.

In the first three months of 1995, the fund rose 18.1%. That's a great performance, although it's not quite as good as Micron Technology, which jumped 85% during the same period. But a year later, when chipmakers swooned, Micron lost 50% of its value in a few months. No mutual funds ever suffer that kind of damage.

Another example might be health maintenance organizations. If you're not sure whether Oxford Health Plans is worth its current price—it is a very controversial stock, with a huge short position—you might prefer to buy a health care fund that has a heavy weighting in many different HMOs.

And funds probably represent the best way to invest abroad. It's pretty difficult for someone in California or Kentucky to follow closely the workings of a company that is headquartered in Switzerland, Hong Kong, or Malaysia. A professional money manager can help.

The diversification a mutual fund offers is even more important when you invest internationally. If you own just two or three international stocks, you face an extraordinary range of serious risks. As with U.S. stocks, you're subject to market risk (the entire market might drop 25%) and company risk (the company might report bad news). But you're also subject to political risk (the government could be toppled or the president forced to resign because of a scandal) and currency risk (the value of the local currency could fall relative to the dollar, as it did so memorably in Mexico in 1995).

CHOOSING WINNING FUNDS

If you do decide to put some of your money in mutual funds, there's no reason to settle for mediocrity.

Every year, *Individual Investor* selects funds we expect will outperform their peers. And we've been pretty good at it. In 1994, for instance, we chose two of the three biggest winners—out of more than 5,000 mutual funds.

Here are the steps we take—and the ones you can follow—to find the top performers.

First, consult resources such as *Morningstar*, the *Value Line Mutual Fund Survey*, and leading business and personal finance magazines

(*Money, Worth, Forbes, SmartMoney,* and so on) to determine the top performers for the previous year. Then use the same sources—or data from *The Wall Street Journal* or *Investor's Business Daily*—to see which of the funds have been particularly strong in the past six months.

The goal is to find a talented fund manager in whose strategy you believe. How long a track record are you looking for? Here's where I disagree with many mutual fund analysts. I think there's more danger in being late than in being early.

One of the great enemies of hot mutual funds is success. After outperforming the market for three years or more, money starts to flow in from the public by the cartload. Soon, the fund is so much larger than it was when it achieved its initial success that, in essence, it typically becomes a very different fund.

Example: a $50 million small-cap fund that balloons to a billion dollars in assets will find it has to seek out larger, better-known companies to invest in. But its niche had been investing in microscopic companies no one had ever heard of (the kind discussed throughout this book). The fund *could* continue to achieve the same levels of success. But in the real world, that hardly ever happens.

When assessing a mutual fund, recent rapid asset growth is almost always a negative.

This argument doesn't mean we ignore a fund's longer-term track record entirely. We do care whether a manager has dramatically outperformed the market over the past three years. The five-year performance record, however, is of much less interest.

FLUKES IN FUNDS

Nonetheless, in focusing on more recent performance, you always have to be on the lookout for flukes. The best performing fund in the United States in the final quarter of 1993, for instance, was a very tiny ($10 million) fund that had compiled a consistently atrocious performance record up until that very moment. Was there a reason to think that the great quarter represented a remarkable turning point for the fund?

No. It looked like plain dumb luck. Given the chronic ineptitude of the fund's 75-year-old manager, it was a good bet that he would once again begin underperforming the market. Which is exactly what he did in 1994.

After putting together a list of twelve strong funds in five different categories, our staff must then winnow that down to just three funds in each category. Performance records have helped bring us to this point, but from here on the numbers—by themselves—don't tell you what you need to know.

First, we get the fund's annual report, to determine its mandate. Warning to readers: Mutual fund annual reports are among the worst-written documents in America. Slightly less riveting than VCR manuals, they seem designed *not* to be read. Still, if you stay awake, they can give you a clear sense of the fund's mission.

A less painful route might be to go directly to *Morningstar, Value Line,* and financial magazines to learn what screens various fund managers rely on to select stocks. But don't trust that the fund's name will necessarily give you a good sense of its buy-and-sell criteria. The Seligman Communications Fund is not really a communications fund at all. It's a technology fund.

Some technology funds, on the other hand, might really be communications or semiconductor funds. Which might be good, or bad. It depends on your outlook for the sector and the makeup of your existing portfolio.

Before buying a fund, you need to understand: (1) what the manager is trying to do; (2) how he or she is attempting to accomplish this goal; and (3) what kind of portfolio management philosophy is driving the transactions.

You can start by looking at the composition of a fund's portfolio. How many stocks does the manager own? How big a bet is being made on any one sector or any single company? What is the average P/E ratio of the portfolio? What is the annual turnover in holdings?

Is the manager a momentum player or has he or she shown a gift for getting into attractive stocks well ahead of the crowd? (If I see, for instance, that a manager bought Stratacom, Atmel, and other hot stocks way before the rest of the pack, I'm definitely impressed. This suggests that the manager has both a good understanding and a good feel for technology issues—attributes that should lead to more big winners in the future.)

To make sure that we understand and respect a fund's approach, we call and interview the fund manager. Can you do the same? Sometimes. It won't always work, but if you sound intelligent and polite, and don't demand too much of the manager's time, you may get through.

In many cases, even if you can't talk directly to the fund manager, you can get updated information on the portfolio's five largest holdings. This information—which might have been updated on the day you call—will be more current than the numbers reported by the research services.

The goal here is to go behind the numbers—and behind the name—to analyze a manager's approach. One of the reasons we liked the Seligman Communications Fund so much was that our interview with manager Paul Wick convinced us that he was playing technology in a very intelligent way.

Wick's fund was making a big bet on companies whose products would allow the communications revolution to take place, such as chipmakers and semiconductor equipment companies. But he was shunning direct bets on wireless communications companies, having concluded that some were overpriced and others were too risky.

This creative, coolly reasoned approach to technology made sense to us. We thought we understood why his plan would work. Even if Wick's bearish view of the cash-flow-negative wireless communications stocks turned out to be overdone, he would make money because the suppliers to those concerns would flourish.

The result? Seligman Communications A was the top performer among all American mutual funds in 1994, rising 35% (or 33.8% more than the S&P 500).

One of our other choices for best aggressive growth fund was the Govett Smaller Companies Fund. In 1993, its first year, the fund racked up a remarkable gain of 58.5%. Many fund-pickers might automatically avoid a fund this young, but we're more aggressive. We also knew that manager Garrett Van Wagoner had been a small-cap portfolio manager for more than ten years, so he knew the territory. And our analysis of his approach convinced us that he might be able to outperform the market once again.

And boy, did he! The fund was up 29% in a year when the average equity mutual fund rose only 2%.

What made us back Van Wagoner? We thought he had a hot hand for a very good reason. Actually, his approach isn't so different from the one I advocate in this book.

First, Van Wagoner specializes in underfollowed small-cap companies (the average market cap of stocks in his portfolio is $350 million). And he applies the PEG ratio much as we do. He looks for companies that will grow earnings by at least 20% for the next three years and he'll only buy them if they're selling for a multiple that is less than their projected growth rate. (Now, by the way, he does this work under his own umbrella, as head of the newly formed Van Wagoner Funds Family.)

RULES FOR MUTUAL FUND BUYERS

1. If one of your funds begins to underperform the market, get a sense of *why* this is occurring. During some periods, aggressive growth funds will underperform value funds or big-cap funds. That's inevitable. Of greater concern, however, is how your aggressive growth fund is performing versus its peers. If a once-hot fund starts to lag its direct competitors, consider dumping it after a quarter or two.

As a rule, aggressive growth funds that hit a slump should be jettisoned much faster than value funds that hit a dry patch.

2. Don't rule out funds with front-end loads. All things being equal, I prefer no-load funds. But all things are seldom equal. Both

Seligman Communications and Govett Smaller Companies, for example, have front-end loads. When a fund is hot, the load will seem a small price to pay.

Besides, a load fund may actually be cheaper, over time, than a no-load fund with high expenses and fees. The no-load Kauffmann fund has a total expense ratio of 2.8%. Some funds with 4% or 5% loads have annual expenses of well under 2%. That means that, after three years, the costs of owning the two funds may be almost identical.

3. Your quest to find some of the best funds could help you in another way. Let's say you've found two or three fund managers with excellent recent records and a style you appreciate. If you notice that two of the managers recently began buying the same stock—or added heavily to existing positions—you might want to do your own research into that company. The odds are good that it will be a winner.

Looking for great funds will often lead you to terrific individual stock ideas—you keep your eyes open.

You might come across such information while screening for funds in the formal manner discussed above, or via a more direct route. One valuable daily feature of *Investor's Business Daily* is a list of six top-performing mutual funds and their ten largest holdings (it's usually on page B2). The list also notes the funds' largest recent buy-and-sell decisions in particular stocks.

Even if you never buy a mutual fund, analyzing top mutual fund managers can help turn you into a much better stock-picker.

9

When to Sell

I wish I knew when to sell a stock.

Deciding whether to unload a stock you loathe or love may be the hardest thing an investor has to do.

If you've ever invested, you probably know how agonizing and surprisingly emotional the idea of selling can be. One day you want out. The next day you don't. It's so hard to be decisive. The thought of selling transforms most investors into Hamlet.

Everyone fears that a stock sold today will begin an unprecedented parabolic ascent tomorrow. Or, alternately, that if one decides to stay the course with a lagging or beaten-down stock, it will remain a dog and never have its day.

All investors have trouble selling, but, for some, it's especially difficult. Why? Because they know that they will never get back into a stock once they unload it. The key reason: The psychological cost of admitting that they were wrong is simply too high.

There is a much more productive way to view this situation. Become more detached. Tell yourself that it's OK—in fact, it can be downright smart—to repurchase a stock someday if the reasons you sold it no longer apply.

SELL SYSTEMS

The fact that selling is so difficult has led both professionals and amateurs to search for a mechanical system to handle the messy business. William O'Neil, publisher of *Investor's Business Daily*, may have the lowest loss tolerance of anyone who has created a selling system. He believes in dumping a stock the second it falls 7% below the purchase price. Others advocate putting in stop-loss orders at prices 10%, 15%, or 20% below the entry point.

I have two primary objections to such mechanical methods. First, with some small-cap stocks, a 7% move can be absolutely inconsequential. Such fluctuations don't tell you much. They're usually nothing but noise.

Unfortunately, that's not how a sell system processes such data. In this case, a system may force you to sell prematurely for no good reason at all.

My second objection is more basic. I am faced with sell/hold decisions constantly, and I've never found a mechanical approach that improves my performance. On the contrary, I think that one of the ways to lose money with small caps is to sell too soon—whether after a slight decline or following a modest run-up.

If you really think that a stock could be a huge winner, you have to give it a little room to move. That's the only way a positive scenario has a chance to play out. Otherwise, you may make some extraordinarily expensive mistakes. Imagine selling Microsoft in 1986 because it had a few down days. You could have left thousands of percentage points of profits on the table.

Another argument against mechanical selling systems is that, in the short run, any stock—not just a small cap—can be highly volatile and fake you out in either direction. Such moves don't necessarily have any long-term implications.

Nonetheless, stop orders have value for some investors. If you know that, on occasion, you cannot sell a stock no matter what happens, then a stop-loss system may work well for you. Similarly, if you are either a conservative or a very nervous investor, a mechanical system might be smart. It certainly achieves two goals: (1) limiting potential losses and (2) helping you sleep at night. As for maximizing your returns, I think that's another story.

Blindly following a sell system suggests that you don't really know your stock. That's why the first thing I do when a stock moves sharply *isn't* to sell or to buy. It's to demand an explanation. A price decline is a signal to perform due diligence all over again, which is exactly what you should—and really can—do.

Here's an example that hits very close to home. It concerns Individual Investor Group (INDI), the publisher of *Individual Investor* magazine. I happen to be the chairman.

In the second half of October 1995, the stock market realized that we would not extend the life of two series of our warrants (securities that are broadly analogous to options), which were due to expire in November and could be converted into INDI stock at $3.50 and $4 per share, respectively. In the short run, the market reasoned, this would put pressure on our stock.

Why? For two reasons, neither of which was particularly compelling for long-term investors. First, when warrants are converted into common shares, the number of shares outstanding rises. A warrant conversion is dilutive to earnings. (But, since it is public knowledge that the warrants exist and can be converted someday, this is hardly news.)

Second, with INDI trading at $6, it was inevitable that some investors would convert the warrants into common shares and then quickly sell the stock. That would probably put some short-term pressure on our shares. This became another negative in the minds of some investors.

What happened? In seven trading days in October, INDI was hammered from $6 to $4.38. The initial selling (sometimes on high volume) led to more selling by investors, who naturally figured something was amiss at a company whose stock was falling every day during a bull market. By November 10, the stock was down to $4.13.

If an investor had taken the time to call us, we would have explained the warrants situation and informed them that business had never been better. Unfortunately, hardly anyone called. The story didn't make the newspapers—we're a very small company—so shareholders were completely in the dark unless they had a broker who followed INDI closely.

As our stock price tumbled, some investors with mechanical sell systems undoubtedly got out. At $5.50. Or $4.88. Or $4.38. Or $4.13. Which is sad, considering that the actual news about the warrants was neutral. The stock fell 27% in seven trading sessions, and 31% in four weeks. This was an example of a short-term buying opportunity for investors who understood what was going on.

Just seven weeks after trading at $4.13, INDI zoomed 70% to $7, an all-time high.

The moral: A price decline means that someone is dumping the stock, but it certainly doesn't mean that the dumper is right. If you know the company well, then your opinion matters. If you're honest with yourself about why you continue to hold—or buy—when others are rushing to sell, then you can buck the market. The market can be wrong, and the best investors profit from its inefficiency and occasional irrationality.

When one of your stocks starts falling, here's what to do:

- Call the company and ask tough questions. If sales growth has slowed or earnings have declined, try to get a sense of how long the problem will last.

- Hit the "news" button on a computer (do this online or have your broker do it). Ask your full-service broker to make some calls about the stock.

- Call the company's underwriter. Some problems won't show up as news items, but will be known on the Street. Perhaps a negative rumor is circulating or there are whispers that a competitor may have a hot new product in the works.

LETTING YOUR WINNERS RUN

One reason I have been successful is that I really follow the old Wall Street wisdom of letting my winners run. Just as I don't believe in sell systems, I also don't believe in price targets. I don't think you should sell when a stock rises 25%, 50%, or 200%. Like many pieces of old-time investing wisdom—buy low/sell high comes to mind—this is much easier said than done.

Reasons to Sell

- Deteriorating fundamentals. This is a Wall Street abbreviation for saying the reasons you bought the stock no longer seem to apply. Something significant has changed—for the worse.

Serious signs of danger are numerous. Look for them and be aware of their potential effects.

1. Inventories are growing faster than sales. A fast-growing company should see strong gains in both sales and inventory. When inventory is rising faster, it suggests that the company has miscalculated customer demand or is having trouble selling items that are now out of favor (this could apply to out-of-fashion clothes, technology that has been superseded, or similar items that are hard to move).

2. It's taking longer to collect receivables. This usually means that customers are dissatisfied with recent shipments or uncertain about their quality. It could also tell you that customers are having cash-flow difficulties, which is a two-pronged problem: (a) your company may not be getting paid for some goods shipped and (b) the industry served by your company may be having serious problems.

3. There's no compelling reason to expect things to change. It's essential for a good investor to understand the concept of opportunity cost. Technically, this "cost" refers to the highest alternate guaranteed rate of return you could earn by parking your money elsewhere, rather than in Joe's Co. (or any particular investment). It may be costing you 6% a year, say, to hold on to your shares in Joe's Co.

I find that technical definition too lenient. For my purposes, opportunity cost is the return of the overall stock market or my personal average annual return.

You can illustrate this concept with hundreds and hundreds of case histories. One is Ryan's Family Steakhouse, a profitable southern chain of steak joints. Ryan's stock was trading at $7 in 1987. In February 1996, Ryan's was still trading at $7.

What had happened? Nothing much—and that's the problem. In most of the intervening quarters, Ryan's made money. It just never showed any ability to grow its earnings.

So how were patient, profit-hungry investors rewarded? Ryan's pays no dividend, so they received no help there. In short, $10,000 invested in Ryan's in 1987 is worth (before inflation) $10,000 today. This investment has been a bit like putting money in a mattress that happens to be publicly traded.

As for the opportunity cost, the S&P 500 rose approximately 160% over the same period, which means that the owner of an S&P 500 fund would have seen $10,000 become $26,000. That's $16,000 more than the Ryan's holder would have, and that buys a lot of steak. By my calculations, the patient holder of Ryan's stock lost $16,000 in nine years on a $10,000 investment.

For serious investors, that's the way the math should be done. It is far too kind to say that Ryan's really went nowhere. It went South big-time, when you factor in opportunity cost, not to mention inflation.

The lesson: When you own companies in traditional industries (restaurants, retail, manufacturing, and insurance, among others), you must be ruthless about demanding improved results soon. Maybe not this year, but certainly next year. Waiting indefinitely almost guarantees that you will create a self-inflicted wound.

How fast should you bail out? If the company misses its numbers once, that's a tough call (see above). When it misses them again, get rid of the turkey.

Realize, though, that such impatience can be inappropriate with some young companies in biotech or high-tech. When you buy stock in companies that will realize the bulk of their earnings in the future, it is foolish to sell in six months because the earnings expected in 2002 didn't materialize yet.

4. Sometimes, life hands you a high-class problem. You own a stock that has doubled or tripled—or sextupled—within a relatively short period—let's say, a year or less. What do you do?

At the risk of contradicting what I said earlier (prudently assess whether the stock still represents good value today, and then act accordingly), I would usually sell some. If my $10,000 investment has tripled to $30,000, I might sell a third of my stake, thus converting $10,000 back into cash.

This lets me recoup the value of my original investment, but the profits I've made stay invested. And I still have a substantial stake in the stock—$20,000 worth, or twice as much as I was originally willing to risk.

This strategy has great psychological and financial value to me. It helps me hold a stock when things look dicey. Because I've lowered the amount of money I'm risking, I find it easier to hang tough during the inevitable market turbulence.

On the other hand, I know many investors who sell too early because they are terrified that their profits—which took months or years to build—might disappear in a flash. They panic the first time the stock drops, and they miss out on some enormous future gains.

Their fear is perfectly understandable and almost universal. There are few things worse in life than buying a stock at $10, watching it run to $30, and then selling it at $7.38. (Yes, one thing *is* worse: having to tell someone you love that you actually did this.)

Banking some of your winnings is a great way of overcoming this fear. After selling a portion of your holdings, you can manage the remainder more dispassionately. Your ultimate decision to hold or sell will be based less on emotion and more on the information at hand.

5. When you see fraud or dishonesty. The difficult part here is trying to tell the difference between bad business practices and outright chicanery. Media Vision, one of our worst stock picks ever, played games with the books to inflate the stock price. When the

news became public, we told readers to sell at $4, even though the price had been more than ten times higher just a few months earlier.

We advocated selling at that point because we knew things could get much worse. Earnings would have to be restated for years, loan covenants would be violated, customer loyalty might disintegrate, bankruptcy proceedings might begin, and so on. The only thing absolutely knowable was that something was rotten at the company.

Later, Media Vision did indeed file for bankruptcy. A few months after our admittedly belated sell advice, Media Vision shares stopped trading altogether. Note: A 90% decline in a stock's price is likely to represent a selling rather than a buying opportunity. Stocks that fall so far so fast are often heading straight for oblivion.

Consider a counterexample, however. In 1992, Oracle Corporation, already a high flier, plunged from about $40 to around $15 after it was revealed that the company was booking sales more aggressively than it should have. It was a management and public relations disaster, but the company's products and services remained sound.

Oracle made management, accounting, and sales policy changes. Meanwhile, the company's phenomenal growth continued. From a low of about $10, Oracle shares rose to $53.25 in 1996.

My rule here is to hold on when the products are good, necessary management changes have been made, and the people in charge are not corrupt. I won't stick around, though, if:

- The company fires its auditors and/or lawyers. Only at an honest company can you expect that management will take care of its shareholders instead of enriching its own coffers.

- Managers who have lost their credibility remain in place. If you know a company's top management is dishonest, you have to get out immediately. Either they'll rob you blind or you will never know what's actually going on—or both.

- Overvaluation occurs.

Regarding overvaluation, sometimes too much good news is bad news. That's what caused us to get out of MicroTouch Systems in

November 1994 at $40.25, a price 353% higher than our $8.88 entry point two years earlier.

MicroTouch, the world's leading maker of touch screens for computers and kiosks, is a fine company. What spooked us was not the stock's enormous price rise per se, but the fact that, at its high, MicroTouch had a market cap of more than $300 million. That's a large valuation for a company that dominates a fairly small market niche and has few immediate prospects of expanding into other markets.

Furthermore, we felt that MicroTouch's wide profit margins, which helped produce its high market cap, would cause more competitors to enter the field. That might not be terrible news, but it couldn't be good.

We unloaded before anything negative happened. And then the disappointments began. The company failed to make its numbers several times.

The lesson: When you own a hot stock, always ask whether it seems to be ahead of itself. What kind of growth and future profitability does the market cap promise? Is this reasonable to you? With MicroTouch, we concluded that touch screens were a nice small business but would not significantly affect the future of computing. This was a good growth story but not a great one, and the current stock price more than adequately reflected the company's near-term profit potential.

6. You find something better. Without driving yourself crazy, you should reassess the prospects of your stocks constantly. Every day, I wake up and ask, "Are these the stocks to own or not?" I'm always trying to upgrade my holdings. One of the most basic ways is to look for a company in the same business that is growing faster or is selling for a lower multiple—or both.

You don't have wait for bad news to sell. If you lose confidence in a company and don't feel comfortable holding it, that is reason enough to say farewell. I believe in holding a stock only as long as you can see a catalyst that is likely to make it move. It could be a new product, impending FDA approval, or the prospect of great earnings. But if you don't see any of those things, maybe you should move on.

REASONS NOT TO SELL

1. Because investor X bails out. Many people think that when a savvy investor dumps a stock it is a sign to head for the exit as well. Often, this is simply not true.

2. It's especially untrue when the professional investor in question is doing nothing abnormal. Consider venture capitalists who cash out of a stock after a 500%, 1,000%, or 1,500% gain. Selling at this point is their job. They need to put that money to work elsewhere.

Does this make them bearish on the stock they're selling? Hardly. The returns sought by most venture capitalists—40% to 50% a year—are almost impossible to achieve by holding a portfolio of publicly traded stocks. The only way to realize such returns is to back a company when it is very young and privately held.

Example: In 1995, McAfee Associates announced a secondary public offering. All the shares were being sold by a terrific California venture capital firm with a gift for spotting winners early.

On the day of the offering, McAfee actually rose $2 to $25. Then it quickly ran up to $32. A few months later it hit $56.25.

So were the super-smart venture capitalists wrong? Not really. It is quite possible that they used their McAfee proceeds as seed money for one of the next century's great winners.

When a major holder turns into a seller, try to understand why. If it is a venture capitalist, don't worry. If it is a major corporation, don't fret either. (Most corporations invest so badly that you would be better off doing the opposite of what they do.) You should be concerned only when the seller is a highly successful stock market investor whose moves have been worth emulating over the years.

Warren Buffett, for instance, was a big owner of advertising agency stocks in the 1970s and early 1980s, correctly seeing them as a great inflation play. As inflation waned, Buffett sold his holdings. The group has been a laggard ever since.

Sometimes, though, it's very hard to hold on to a stock when a prominent critic says you're being a fool. In a 1995 issue of *Barron's*, a well-known technology investor said he had become bearish on the entire tech sector. Traders reacted by shellacking the tech stocks he owned, and they especially brutalized those in which he had made a form 13D filing. (Investors who own at least 5% of a company must file form 13D with the SEC.)

Among those form 13D holdings was CMGI, one of the largest positions in my own hedge fund.

In the weeks after the article's appearance, CMGI was cut in half, plunging from $19.50 to $10. The carnage began because traders thought that investors would be unloading their shares and some *Barron's* readers bailed out. Then the early selling created its own downward momentum.

In a matter of weeks, more than half of our profit went up in smoke. Anyone with a brain would have thought of selling.

We did think about it. But before unloading, we revisited the fundamentals. Was the story still unfolding as we had hoped? Yes. First, the Internet seemed to represent ongoing value. Second, we learned from the company and from analysts that CMGI's key components were still doing well. Basically, little had changed other than the stock price.

Our conclusion: We thought we knew the CMGI story at least as well as anyone else did, and we believed the selling had been overdone. Furthermore, we hadn't really learned anything negative about the company, except for the fact that one of its major investors had recently soured on the entire technology universe. That was information worth knowing—after all, it helped explain the dreadful decline we were experiencing—but it wasn't necessarily relevant to the future earnings power of CMGI.

Instead of selling out, we used the decline to buy more CMGI shares. Over the next six months, the stock rose 400%.

2. A product or order delay. This happens to almost every company at some point. One of the great stocks of my lifetime—Microsoft—is notorious for missing product shipment deadlines.

(In fact, rivals have accused Microsoft of announcing unrealistic shipping dates as a strategy for crushing competitors.) Selling Microsoft early because its products were late would not have been very smart.

In the third quarter of 1995, IBM announced that $350 million of expected mainframe sales would not come through until the fourth quarter. In little more than a week's time, the stock fell from a high above $100, all the way down to $82. Four months later, it was back up to $122.

This example doesn't prove that it pays to be complacent about all delays. Far from it. But it does suggest that when you learn about a delay, it is time to do more research.

Try to ascertain the reason behind the delay. Is the product delayed because the market has shifted (bad news) or because it has a few bugs in it (not bad news)? Is the company having trouble getting the price it wants for the product as presently configured (bad news) or is the firm just trying to improve the design (not so bad)?

In the case of an order delay, find out whether the sales will be lost forever or will merely be booked a few months late. Will a competitor swoop in and steal the sales or are the company's customers loyal to its offerings?

3. When the company you own is the market leader. This, at least, is a reason to consider holding on. Market leaders have enormous benefits in pricing, distribution, and customer loyalty. That doesn't mean market leadership makes anyone invincible or all-powerful, but it does help a company withstand some temporary setbacks.

Ask the normal questions about earnings expectations and the fundamentals of the business. And be sure you know whether Company X is still a leader or is living off its former glory. A tremendous amount of money can be lost by holding on to yesterday's heroes.

4. The stock is performing beautifully. Let's discuss letting your winners run in more detail. There are at least three enemies of this sound policy: (1) timidity ("It's up so much it probably can't go any higher"), (2) fear ("Any day, it's going to turn around and head

back to where I bought it"), and (3) the opinions of other people ("Sell already! Don't be greedy.").

If you're smart enough or lucky enough to be holding a big winner, keep these key principles in mind:

- Great stocks are relatively rare. Once you've found one, try hard not to let go.

- The more your stock rises, the more negative things you will start to hear about it. Short-sellers will target it. Journalists may wonder whether the stock hasn't moved too far too fast. Investors who never owned it will be upset about their oversight and will bad-mouth the stock's prospects. Investors who did own the stock, but sold too soon, will say almost anything negative to justify their mistake to themselves. Don't get coaxed out of a great investment because of what people say.

- Treat a big winner like any other stock. Don't be overeager to sell. Believe me, if you are too eager to sell, the market will eventually give you a reason and you'll sell your stock at the wrong time.

- Constantly reevaluate the stock. Although I don't set explicit targets, I do set goals based on how I think a company will perform in the next two years. When I analyze quarterly earnings and news items, I adjust these expectations. I'm always aware of a stock's current P/E multiple and its multiple based on next year's expected earnings.

- Be prepared for volatility. When small-cap stocks tumble, the fall can be stomach-churning. Cope by keeping your eye on the big picture—the long-term prospects of the company, the reason you bought in the first place, the business fundamentals as you know them.

CMGI, mentioned earlier, is a textbook case of a volatile stock that has given nervous investors endless opportunities to exit prematurely, while providing knowledgeable buyers with ample reentry points at bargain prices.

Just because we bought heavily after a sharp pullback doesn't mean it is inappropriate to ever sell some of the stock. As CMGI, post-*Barron's* debacle, went from $10 to $50.25, we did take some profits. At an average price of $35 per share, we sold about 30% of our stake. One reason we sold was that the huge appreciation in the stock—our original purchase price was $4—had caused it to account for too high a percentage of our portfolio.

In January 1996, the stock of Vtel Corporation, a videoconferencing company, was hammered from $17 to $10 on an earnings disappointment. Even before investigating the causes of the shortfall, my reflex was to hold the stock—for three reasons. First, Vtel is a fine company (backed by Intel) in a rapidly growing business. Second, videoconferencing sales are seasonal. (The more seasonal a business, the more patience you should have with a bad earnings announcement.) Third, the stock could rebound 20% in two days simply because the selling was overdone. I could always sell then if I decided to get out.

As it happened, further research supported our faith in Vtel. Within six weeks, the stock was back at $13.

5. Because you have to sell. This is a terrible reason for selling, and it indicates poor planning or recklessness somewhere along the line.

To become a wise seller, you have to structure your financial life so you have staying power in the market. To begin with, that means not investing your rent money. In addition, it means that you shouldn't be heavily margined, particularly if your portfolio consists of only one, two, or three stocks.

In this case, you may be forced to sell regardless of the stock's fundamentals. Or, you may feel so much pressure that it's almost impossible to make the right decision.

In investing, the more pressure you feel, the more likely that you'll make a mistake. Selling intelligently is tough enough without adding financial pressure to the equation. You need to be calm, analytical, and rational to do it well—and even then it's quite a challenge.

10

The Information Age

We are in the midst of a financial information explosion, and that's great news for investors. Reliable, up-to-the-minute information on stocks and mutual funds can lead to bigger profits in the market. Software programs and online services can help you become an outstanding investor.

Alas, some investors now find themselves suffering from an intense case of information overload. They're having trouble processing all the nifty new data they have at their fingertips. They have so much data that they succumb to analysis paralysis. Instead of becoming twenty-first-century investors, they've become numb.

There's a simple way out of this muddle. Figure out what information-gathering approach works best for you. What fits your budget? What can your schedule accommodate? What investment of time and money actually improves your market results?

Don't forget to ask some questions that have nothing to do with money directly. Which information sources are the most fun to use? Which do the best job of teaching you about the investing issues most important to you?

I can recommend good resources and tell you what I rely on, but I can only give you suggestions about what might work for you. With that in mind, let's begin with a few guidelines that should apply to almost everybody.

Rules of Engagement

1. Use information in moderation. Spend an amount commensurate with the size of your portfolio. You could easily spend thousands of dollars annually accumulating information and crunching numbers, but that's a crazy outlay for the average investor.

If you have a job and a family, and thus have only a few hours a week to devote to investing, it makes little sense to spend a fortune on information resources. Great information you never use has no value.

Apply the same logic that you'd bring to buying, or canceling, a premium cable-TV service. How much do you use a particular resource? Which one gives you the biggest bang for the buck? Is there a cheaper way to get the same data?

If you're spending money on a resource, use it—or scrap it.

2. Start small. Find out what your information intake tolerance is. Slowly decide how in-depth and technical you want your approach to be. Don't ever sign up for anything simply to impress your friends—or yourself.

3. Sample. Take advantage of trial offers for magazines, newsletters, research services, and online information sources. This is a cheap way to get to know a range of products. Don't feel pressured to commit to a specific system today just because you're reading this book or because a friend is euphoric about the latest $100-a-month information marvel.

A good way to sample newsletters: Select Information Exchange (244 West 54th Street, New York, NY 10019; 800-743-9346) offers very inexpensive trial subscriptions to four or more newsletters simultaneously. You buy by the batch, but the cost is often lower than many individual trial subscriptions.

4. Think. Beware of what happens to some investors who go online. I'm not talking here about high monthly access charges, although that is an important point by itself. My concern is with how you use instant information. There's a right way and a wrong way.

Some online investors feel compelled to act the second new information appears. Sometimes that's smart, but often it isn't. Don't let the speed of the information flow lead to hasty decisions.

If you're a trader, of course, reaching quick decisions may be essential. But if you're a long-term investor, it's important to take your time, no matter how furious the flow of new information. Before acting on news, always try to ascertain whether the information you have has worked its way into the consciousness of other investors. Remember, you're not the only one who is getting information faster these days.

What I Do

Although I have a research staff, several Bloomberg terminals (a high-end, online news service for professionals), and access to expensive monthly data and analysis services, I still love many information sources that are probably well within your means.

The *Wall Street Journal*

It is my deep conviction that a weekday morning without the *Wall Street Journal* is like a day without sunshine. I've been addicted since I was a teenager, and I have no desire to join a twelve-step program that will help me quit.

The *Journal* provides excellent background on business and economic trends, although I don't consider it a stock-picking resource per se. But it can help you pinpoint worthwhile investment themes and, indirectly, lead to some great investment ideas.

Investor's Business Daily

IBD is a great stock-picking and research tool. It offers stock market tables you can't find anywhere else. IBD calls them "intelligent" tables, and the adjective is well-deserved.

Here's what you get:

- EPS rank. This measures the growth and stability of a company's earnings over the past five years, with special emphasis on growth in the preceding two quarters. IBD uses a 1-to-99 percentile scale, so the fastest-growing companies will be ranked 80 or higher.

- Relative price strength. The idea here is simple. On the same 1-to-99 scale, a company's stock performance over the past twelve months is compared to every other stock in the IBD universe. This is a momentum indicator. When possible, I prefer to buy stocks whose relative strength has recently been improving. It's a good sign when the ranking is 80 to 95 or so.

  I'm less comfortable when the ranking is in the very high 90s. If it's 99, that means the stock has outperformed 99% of all other stocks during the past year. It has been a very big winner. (Actually, it may have outperformed 99.99% of all stocks.) The winning streak may continue, but I think you have to ask, "Am I too late on this one?"

- Volume percentage change. This tells you how the preceding day's volume in a stock compares to its average daily trading volume over the previous fifty trading days. A big price move in either direction probably doesn't mean much if it occurs on low volume. The higher the volume, the more significant the move probably is.

- Industry group relative strength. Every stock is part of an industry group. This group ranking, which appears each Monday, compares the performance of a stock's group with 196 other groups. An A ranking means the group is in the top 20%; a B puts it in the top 40%; and so on.

  The grade tells you whether the group is in favor. Generally, I like to buy into groups that are doing well. If the stock's group is in the doghouse, that helps explain why the stock might have a weak relative strength ranking.

- Sponsorship rank. This ranking, which appears every Wednesday, averages the three-year performance history of all mutual funds owning the stock. It's better if the smartest mutual fund managers, and not the dumbest, have a position in the stock. After all, which club would you rather join?

- Owned by management. Every Thursday, IBD tells you what percentage of shares outstanding are owned by management. My view is, the higher the better. That's why we include the percentage in our stock articles in *Individual Investor*.

Once past the stock tables, you'll encounter valuable features. Every day, IBD prints charts and detailed information on 66 stocks over $12 that hit new highs the previous day or are currently near new highs. Again, this fits into our momentum theory that the new highs list is a great place to go stock-shopping, and the new lows list should be avoided like the plague.

IBD's earnings coverage is the finest of any daily or weekly. A list of companies reporting the best (up at least 20%) and worst earnings appears daily. For a fairly active investor who is serious about buying some of America's fastest-growing companies, this can be a great time-saver. Even if you already subscribe to *Individual Investor*, IBD's earnings coverage can supplement your research and give you more timely information.

Finally, the paper's New America page profiles three of the fastest-growing companies in the country. Almost without exception, these companies have already been picked by the earnings growth screens used by IBD and by *Individual Investor*. The stories can help give you a sense of how much rapid growth might remain.

Value Line Investment Survey

Value Line has helped me as an investor since high school, although I now use it differently. I used to care passionately about the survey's timeliness rankings, and there's no reason that you shouldn't. Value Line stocks ranked 1 or 2 (out of 5) have beaten the market handily for more than 30 years.

I generally ignore the rankings, for two reasons. First, relatively few of the companies Value Line tracks are small caps. Second, I'm arrogant enough to think that I can determine a stock's timeliness ranking at least as well as Value Line.

So why do I still pay attention? Because Value Line's one-page reports on individual companies are fantastic. They give you an awesome amount of data, including multiyear tables of sales, earnings, profit margins, and more—an excellent profile of where a company has been and where it might be headed.

Dick Davis Digest

This is a terrific and probably underrated resource. Essentially, it is the *Reader's Digest* of market newsletters, offering recommendations and excerpts from over 400 different letters every two weeks. I love it because I can see some of my peers' best ideas without having to wade through thousands of pages every month.

What's the value of seeing how others think? You can make money by understanding what appeals to some of the smartest investors out there. Maybe I'll learn that someone else has discovered a company with a new way to profit from the growth of the Internet. Perhaps several of the newsletter writers I respect most are interested in the same medical technology company. In either case, their selections might inspire me to do some research.

The Hulbert Financial Digest

Editor Mark Hulbert is the official scorekeeper of the newsletter business. (For the record, he ranks the performance of our *Special Situations Report* but not that of *Individual Investor*.)

I use Hulbert to learn how the competition is doing, to keep tabs on investors I admire, and to figure out which newsletters I should subscribe to.

That last point will be most important for you. Hulbert ranks newsletter writers on both pure performance and risk-adjusted performance. He is scrupulously honest and fair—though some newsletter writers quibble with various points of his methodology—and all his data point to one conclusion.

If you read Hulbert, you'll be less likely to waste money on a newsletter that is probably destined to be more of a handicap than a benefit. Even if you never plan to buy a newsletter, knowing the Hulbert rankings can help. (You can do this for free by reading Hulbert's columns in *Forbes* or thumbing through his book at the library.) When you come upon the stock or market-timing opinions of a self-anointed guru, you'll know how accurate his or her views have been in the past. Consider the alternative: following the advice of someone whose record you know nothing about.

Telescan

Telescan is a software/online package that lets you access and manipulate data in thousands of ways. I can't swear that it's the best system out there, but I do know it's terrific and it works for me. One upfront warning: Telescan is expensive.

I use Telescan to track tick-by-tick changes in the prices of all stocks in my portfolios (the Magic 25 and my hedge fund), as well as those on my watch list. Whenever there is news on one of the stocks, Telescan lets me know.

By pressing a button, I can access Telescan's excellent chart-making capability and then select the period I want the chart to cover (I can go back many years). As you know by now, I'm not a technical analyst, but charts do sometimes help me get a sense of when a stock might be ready to move higher.

I'm particularly impressed with Telescan's stock-screening capabilities, and this might be where an online service could be most valuable for you. Telescan allows you to screen its 7,000-stock universe using dozens of different variables. Among those you might choose are:

- Low P/E ratios.
- Low PEG ratios.

- Low price/sales ratios.

- Rapid sales growth.

- Rapid earnings growth.

- High dividend yields.

- Largest discounts to book value.

Because you can use more than one screen simultaneously, it's easy to generate a list, say, of fast-growing stocks selling at low multiples which have had recent insider buying.

This list will only be a starting point, but it's a great one. Screen wisely and you'll address the investment criteria most important to you and generate some terrific stock ideas. Armed with the list, you can do fundamental research on the stocks that look most attractive.

The computer can be an amazing investment tool. It can create lists of potentially good investment ideas. It provides online access to most of the fundamental information you need (you can download annual reports and press releases directly from some companies). And it stores your research neatly in one place. If you decide to buy a stock, you can do so online, if you wish.

Note: Some products listed at the end of this chapter can provide many of Telescan's services at a lower price. You can, for instance, do Telescan-like stock screening with other services. And you can save money if you don't use up-to-the-minute information. A stock that had a low P/E last month probably still has one today. Consider saving money by using data that are not quite so fresh.

OTHER RECOMMENDED SOURCES

CNBC and CNN FN

You don't need an expensive online service to stay on top of breaking financial news. Both CNBC and CNN FN do a good job of explaining overall market moves. CNBC's interviews with CEOs may lead you to some attractive stocks or industries.

Morningstar

Morningstar is a good service for people who invest a lot of their money in mutual funds. Its rankings and analyses provide valuable information on fund managers' styles, objectives, track records, risk/reward rankings, and current holdings.

Investment Clubs

Joining the right club can help make you a better investor. Being a member can be one of the ways to create an environment that lets you be successful.

Why? Because members will challenge your investment ideas and force you to defend them. I benefit greatly from the give-and-take I have with my research department. And almost every good investor tries to profit from the knowledge and opinions of peers. Professional investors and money managers may boast about how independent-minded they are—and this may be true—but they talk to each other all the time.

A club can be a great source of investment ideas and solid research. Furthermore, it can help you defray the cost of an information service that might be too expensive for you to buy alone (such as Value Line).

Industry-Specific Newsletters

These can be very helpful when you're investing in a particular theme (see Chapter 6). Among those I like is the Sturza Medical Investment Letter, which specializes in biotech and new medical devices. Remember: Some of these outperform the market, but most do not.

ONLINE AND INTERNET SERVICES

Before describing the various online sources of information I use, I should note that, by the time this book is in print, there will be many, many more sources of great information online. The Internet is developing so rapidly, it is literally impossible to keep up. And it would be foolhardy for me to say in a printed book that I have an exhaustive list of all the financial goodies on the Internet. With that as a given, here goes.

Telescan may be a Cadillac online service, but there are many great Chevys out there as well. The major online services—America Online, CompuServe, and Prodigy—all offer 15-minute delayed stock quotes, company profiles, updated market information, and lots of news.

They also offer investor forums, such as AOL's extremely popular Motley Fool. Sometimes, these chat services will provide exciting research leads, as well as interesting perspectives on stocks you own or are considering buying. Besides the potential for profit, the services give you a chance to talk with like-minded investors. One warning: They can be addictive and lead to monthly online bills of $100 or more. Make sure you're getting enough fun or investment value for the money.

The Electronic Wall Street Journal

One of the best services is the online version of the *Wall Street Journal* available on the World Wide Web (http://update.wsj.com).

Essentially, it offers you three enormous benefits:

1. You can receive the online *Journal* early edition about midnight, hours before delivery trucks are loaded with the print edition.

2. Investment information is constantly updated, as are many news stories. The information will often be much fresher than what you can find in print.

3. Because the news hole in cyberspace is virtually limitless, the service contains more in-depth coverage than the print version. Paragraphs that didn't make it into the print *Journal* often show up online.

And you have access to many of the *Journal's* back issues. You can read "Heard on the Street" columns going back several weeks. In the

"Personal Finance" section, you can read articles from the past eighteen months, indexed by subject area.

Every publicly traded company mentioned in that day's *Journal* is hot-linked to background information, such as recent news, stock price performance, earnings, and the balance sheet. Plus, you can search past issues of the *Journal*, get 15-minute delayed quotes, customize your portfolio (as you can with Quicken and other software packages), and receive 24-hour updates on international markets.

THE INTERNET

An incredible amount of investing information is available on the Internet, ranging from primers on mutual funds to extraordinarily technical pieces on derivatives. Let's take a look at some of the better offerings.

- PAWWS (http://pawws.secapl.com/), the Internet subsidiary of the Security APL, a portfolio accounting service, gives investors 15-minute delayed quotes, market information, research, and links to other sites with investment information.

- The American Stock Exchange website (http://www.amex .com/) provides the usual market information and news. but it also has a link to Cambridge Interactive's Investor InTouch site, which offers charts going back a year. There are also 15-minute delayed quotes, company facts, and links to electronic SEC filings for companies listed on the Amex. (Through the Investor InTouch link, you can get this information on 7,000 companies, not just those on the Amex.)

- Fidelity Investments,in its "Investors' Tools" section (http:// www.fid~inv.com8080/), offers an interactive financial planning form far less perfunctory than most. Once you've zeroed in on funds that meet your needs, you can access a wealth of detailed information about them, including Lipper Analytical Services rankings. You can also download the prospectuses for 47 Fidelity funds.

- *Individual Investor Interactive* is available on the World Wide Web (http://www.individualinvestor.com).

MUTUAL FUND INFORMATION

Fund information available through the commercial online services isn't always as detailed as the print versions, but it is far more current. And the time that online services can save in tracking existing funds or hunting for new ideas can be astounding.

Here's what you get from the big three online services.

America Online (AOL)

For $8.95 a month, after a month's free trial, you'll have up to five hours to browse AOL's mutual fund sections. One is managed by Morningstar, and one by the Vanguard Group of Investment Companies, the mutual fund giant.

Those who've read Morningstar's print evaluations may consider its AOL offerings Morningstar Lite. There is a lot of good information here on each fund's performance, fee structure, objectives, and key financial ratios—but in highly distilled form. If you must have all the charts and graphs and nuances of information that characterize the Morningstar Mutual Funds service—not to mention the measured opinion of one of Morningstar's analysts—you won't find the computer offering as filling as you might like.

But what is lacking in detail is made up in currency. The performance data are never much more than a month old, and the portfolio data are updated quarterly. (In print, Morningstar information can be as old as eight months.) Both the online and print versions cover more than 5,700 mutual funds.

Morningstar also offers a slew of Top 25 lists—ranked overall or by objective—for time periods ranging from three months to ten years. If a fund's good performance over the time periods you consider most important catches your eye, you can download the fund profile to your computer for future reference.

Vanguard's information, not surprisingly, is limited to its own fund family. But the section also includes some helpful, if generic, advice on financial planning, as well as some insightful market commentary and investment advice from former Vanguard chairman John Bogle.

Once you're online for more than five hours a month, AOL costs $2.90 per hour.

Prodigy

Prodigy gives you access to both data and advertising. The ads can actually be helpful. A mouse click will get you any prospectus you want—via snail mail—from five fund groups: Dreyfus, Fidelity, Kaufmann, Scudder, and Stagecoach.

With the core Prodigy service, you get the daily close of the 20 largest mutual funds (in the CNBC area), and articles and advice on fund investing (via the electronic version of *Kiplinger's Personal Finance* magazine). Prodigy also features "Mutual Fund Winners," a list of the top five funds in twelve categories for the past year. The list is updated quarterly.

For varying extra charges, Prodigy offers "Mutual Fund Analyzer" and "Tradeline," with charts on fund performance priced at 50 cents each.

CompuServe

CompuServe's service includes "FundWatch Online" by *Money* magazine, a database of 4,800 funds with a format similar to Morningstar's. But rather than provide a menu of multiple Top 25 or Top Five lists, the service offers a sleek search engine that lets you set parameters to screen funds. You can screen for the best-performing funds over the time period of your choice. If you're price-conscious, you can ask to see only funds with no loads, no 12b-1 fees, and barebones expense ratios. If you want to have your cake and eat it too, search for only the top-performing funds that meet your expense criteria.

CompuServe also maintains a section on mutual funds in its investors forum. CompuServe's navigational software is the best of the three major services at letting you compose queries or responses to forum members offline.

If you want to do serious portfolio tracking, including some charting, and you want to do it without paying long-distance charges, your best bet may be to combine a CompuServe subscription with Quicken, Intuit's popular personal-finance program.

NET WORTH

For a cheaper, and arguably better, alternative, consider Galt Technologies' Net Worth, a website.

Galt's designers set out to replicate the best mutual fund features of the big three commercial online services—and then to go them one better. You don't just get an NAV (net asset value) on Net Worth, for example. You get a choice of NAVs, ranging from today's quote to the fund's value on any day within the most recent 120 trading days. The price change is expressed in dollars and cents and as a percentage. The quotes are accompanied by a performance chart. Its span ranges from two weeks to a little more than a year.

A mouse click gets you a fund profile with data from Morningstar. Note: This is the one area in which Galt offers less than its competitors. If Morningstar on AOL is Morningstar Lite, the information on Net Worth is Morningstar Ultralite.

In addition, Galt offers a fund-screening tool that is easier to use than CompuServe's. It lets you set your own parameters for a funds search.

Net Worth also offers full-edition samplers of some top mutual-fund newsletters, including the *Mutual Fund Forecaster* and *Equity Outlook*.

Galt has followed the Prodigy model of mixing information with advertising. While browsing Net Worth, you can order prospectuses for more than 5,000 funds by filling out an online form.

OTHER SOURCES

I can't possibly give you details on every software package and online service that might be helpful, but here, grouped alphabetically by topics, is a list of some of the best investing tools to use with your computer.

Asset Allocation

Macro*World Investment Plan
Macro*World Research Corp.
4265 Brownsboro Road, Suite 170
Winston-Salem, NC 27106-3429
(800) 841-5398

Thinkware
Fidelity Brokerage Services
161 Devonshire Street
Boston, MA 02110
(800) 544-9375

WealthBuilder
Reality Technologies, Inc.
2200 Renaissance Boulevard
King of Prussia, PA 19406
(800) 521-2475 or
(610) 277-7600

Electronic Trading

AccuTrade
4211 S. 102nd Street
Omaha, NE 68127-1031
(800) 535-4444 or
(402) 331-2526

E*Trade
E*Trade Securities, Inc.
480 California Avenue
Palo Alto, CA 94306
(800) 786-2575

Fidelity On-line Xpress
Fidelity Brokerage Services, Inc.
161 Devonshire Street
Boston, MA 02110
(800) 544-9375

Investor Securities Group, Inc.
50 Broad Street
New York, NY 10004
(800) 392-7192

PC Financial Network
One Pershing Place
Jersey City, NJ 07339
(800) 825-5723

QuickWay
Quick & Reilly
26 Broadway
New York, NY 10275
(800) 252-9909

StreetSmart
Charles Schwab & Co.
101 Montgomery Street
San Francisco, CA 94104
(800) 334-4455

Mutual Fund Search

Fund Master TC
Time Trend Software
337 Boston Road
Billerica, MA 01821
(508) 250-3866

Morningstar Mutual Funds
Morningstar, Inc.
225 W. Wacker Drive
Chicago, IL 60606
(800) 876-5005 or
(312) 427-1985

Mutual Fund Search
Telescan, Inc.
10550 Richmond, No .250
Houston, TX 77057
(800) 324-4692 or (713) 952-1060

Portfolio Management

CapTool
TechServe, Inc.
P.O. Box 9
Issaquah, WA 98027
(206) 747-5598

Kiplinger's Simply Money
Computer Associates International, Inc.
One Computer Associates Plaza
Islandia, NY 11788
(800) 225-5224

Managing Your Money
MECA Software, Inc.
55 Walls Drive
Fairfield, CT 06430-5139
(203) 255-1441

Market Manager PLUS
Dow Jones & Co.
P.O. Box 300
Princeton, NJ 08543
(800) 522-3567 or
(609) 520-8349

Money Maker Portfolio
Q-West Associates
P.O. Box 270699
San Diego, CA 92198
(800) 618-6618
(Money Maker Analyzer and Money Maker Chart
    modules available)

NAIC Personal Record Keeper
National Association of Investors Corp.
P.O. Box 220
Royal Oak, MI 46068
(810) 583-6242
(Lower fee for members)

Portfolio Analyzer
Hamilton Software, Inc.
6432 E. Mineral Place
Englewood, CO 80112
(800) 733-9607 or (303) 795-5572

Pulse Portfolio Management System
Equis International
3950 S. 700 East, Suite 100
Salt Lake City, UT 84107
(800) 882-3040

Quicken
Intuit, Inc.
66 Willow Place
P.O. Box 3014
Menlo Park, CA 94026
(800) 524-8742 or (415) 322-0573

Stock Quotes, News, General Information

America Online
8619 Westwood Center Drive
Vienna, VA 22182
(800) 827-6364

BMI
3 Triad Center, Suite 100
Salt Lake City, UT 84180
(800) 255-7374 or (801) 532-3400

CompuServe
P.O. Box 20961
5000 Arlington Center Boulevard
Columbus, OH 43220
(800) 848-8199

Dial Data
Global Market Information, Inc.
56 Pine Street
New York, NY 10005
(800) 367-5968

Dow Jones News/Retrieval
Dow Jones & Co.
P.O. Box 300
Princeton, NJ 08543
(800) 522-3567 or
(609) 520-8349

Microsoft Money for Windows 95
Microsoft Corp.
1 Microsoft Way
Redmond, WA 98052-6399
(800) 426-9400

Prodigy Services Co.
22 North Plains Industrial Highway
Wallingford, CT 06492
(800) 776-3449

Reuters Money Network
Reality Technologies, Inc.
2200 Renaissance Boulevard
King of Prussia, PA 19406
(800) 346-2024 or
(215) 277-7600

Signal
Data Broadcasting Corp.
1900 S. Norfolk Street
San Mateo, CA 94403
(800) 551-1322 or
(415) 571-1800

Telemet America, Inc.
325 First Street
Alexandria, VA 22314
(800) 368-2078 or
(703) 548-2042

Track Online
Global Market Information, Inc.
56 Pine Street
New York, NY 10005
(800) 367-5968

Zacks Investment Research
155 N. Wacker Drive
Chicago, IL 60606
(800) 767-3771 or (312) 630-9880

Stock Selection

CompuServe
P.O. Box 20961
5000 Arlington Center Boulevard
Columbus, OH 43220
(800) 848-8199

Dial Data Retriever Program
Global Market Information, Inc.
56 Pine Street
New York, NY 10005
(800) 367-5968

Dow Jones News/Retrieval
Dow Jones & Co.
P.O. Box 300
Princeton, NJ 08543
(800) 522-3567 or (609) 520-8349

ProSearch
Telescan, Inc.
10550 Richmond, No. 250
Houston, TX 77042
(800) 324-4692 or (713) 952-1060

Stock Selection Guide Toolkit
National Association of Investors Corp.
P.O. Box 220
Royal Oak, MI 46068
(810) 583-6242
(Lower fee for members)

US Equities OnFloppy
Morningstar, Inc.
225 W. Wacker Drive
Chicago, IL 60606
(800) 876-5005 or (312) 427-1985

Value/Screen III
Value Line, Inc.
220 E. 42nd Street
New York, NY 10017-5891

Technical Analysis

Advanced Total Investor
Hughes Financial Services
2 W. Hanover Avenue, Suite 212
Randolph, NJ 07869
(201) 895-5665

AIQ TradingExpert
AIQ Inc.
916 Southwood Boulevard
P.O. Box 7530
Incline Village, NV 89452
(800) 332-2999 or (702) 831-2999

Market Analyzer PLUS
Dow Jones & Co.
P.O. Box 300
Princeton, NJ 08543
(800) 522-3567 or (609) 520-8349

MetaStock
Equis International
3950 S. 700 East, Suite 100
Salt Lake City, UT 84107
(800) 882-3040

NavaPatterns
Nava Development Corp.
251-A Portage Road
Lewiston, NY 14092-1710
(800) 532-0041

Quant IX Portfolio Evaluator
11516 N. Port Washington Road, Suite 206
Milwaukee, WI 53209
(800) 247-6354

SuperCharts
Omega Research
9200 Sunset Drive
Miami, FL 33173
(800) 556-2022 or (305) 270-1095

TeleChart 2000
Worden Brothers, Inc.
4905 Pine Cone Drive, Suite 12
Durham, NC 27707
(800) 776-4940

Telescan Analyzer
Telescan, Inc.
10550 Richmond, No. 250
Houston, TX 77057
(800) 324-4692 or (713) 952-1060

TickerWatcher
Linn Software, Inc.
8641 Pleasant Hill Road
Lithonia, GA 30058
(404) 929-8802

Windows on Wall Street
MarketArts, Inc.
1810 N. Glenville Drive, Suite 124
Richardson, TX 75081
(800) 998-8439

Glossary

Balance sheet A tabulation of assets and of liabilities and share-holders' equity that is part of a company's financial reports. The bottom-line amounts always match. Look here to see how a company is capitalized and how much long- and short-term debt it has. A comparative balance sheet allows you to spot trends in inventories, accounts receivable, and cash on hand, among other items.

Beta The standard measure of a stock's relative volatility. (Some analysts also apply the measure to mutual funds.) This is one way of defining the riskiness of a certain security. The S&P 500 has a beta of 1. Very conservative stocks will usually have betas of less than 1. Stocks that move up and down more dramatically than the overall market have betas greater than 1.

Book value The value of a company's assets, calculated as their cost minus allowances for depreciation. Many value investors like stocks that are trading at close to, or less than, book value. On occasion, however, book value can be illusory. Book value will include the "value" of a plant that makes unwanted products, but the plant has little value until it is updated. Write-offs diminish book value. If any write-offs are looming, the book value number you see is likely to decline.

Cash flow A crucial gauge of corporate health. Cash flow analysis strips away the accounting tricks that can make earnings look better than they really are. Reading the cash flow statement tells you whether a company is generating cash from its operations or hemorrhaging it. An annual cash outflow (a negative cash flow) is common for very young companies, but should set off an alarm with older ones.

Current ratio   A test of a company's ability to meet current obligations with assets on hand. To calculate the ratio, divide a company's total current assets by total current liabilities. A number under 1 should cause concern.

Cyclicals   Stocks whose performance is very closely tied to the strength of the overall economy or to the economics of a particular industry. Such boom-and-bust businesses include aluminum, paper, steel, autos, chemicals, and airlines. With certain rare exceptions, these are not stocks you want to hold forever. You want to buy them early in the cycle or, better yet, before the boom actually starts. When business is booming for your cyclicals, think about selling them.

Debt-to-equity ratio   A company's long-term debt divided by total shareholders' equity. The smaller the number, the better; but figures will vary greatly by industry. Ideally, you'd rather own companies with debt-to-equity ratios that are lower than their peers'. There's less chance that they'll blow up in your face.

Earnings expectations   What people assume future earnings will be, based on company statements or analyst's reports. When more than one analyst follows a company, it's important to know the *consensus* earnings estimate of the group. (Both Zacks Investment Research and I/B/E/S report consensus estimates.) Knowing the expectations helps you value a stock today and reevaluate it after the next earnings report appears.

Earnings surprise   When a company either exceeds or fails to match its earnings expectations. A positive surprise is extremely bullish; a negative shock can be disastrous. In both cases, there's a good chance that the company will surprise again next quarter—in the same direction.

Form 10-K   All public companies must file an annual form 10-K with the SEC. Like an annual report, the document details the company's business and financial condition, but it also addresses risk factors an investor should know. It provides important information not found in an annual report, such as executive salaries, executive incentive plans, covenants with lenders, and pending litigation.

Form 10-Q   One of three forms a company must file quarterly with the SEC. Similar to the quarterly reports you receive in the mail, the form 10-Q provides much more detail, including important disclosures (like the footnotes in an annual report) and data on cash flow.

Form 13-D   An investor or investor group must make a form 13-D filing with the SEC when its ownership stake surpasses 5% of a company. In addition, investors who own more than 5% of a company must file a form 13-D whenever they buy or sell any shares in the company.

   When a great investor makes a form 13-D filing, it can make sense to climb aboard for the ride. It's no sin to piggyback on someone else's terrific idea—as long as you do your homework first.

Income statement   The portion of a company's financial report that reveals key data on sales and costs, and tells how profitable the company has been over a certain period. Ideally, this information will include past profit performance for similar periods. Analyzing and understanding the trends that affect company earnings are essential tasks for serious investors.

Index fund   A fund whose performance is designed to mimic a particular index. When most people hear the term, they immediately think of the S&P 500 index, but funds also track indexes of growth stocks, value stocks, small-cap stocks, and emerging markets, among others. Such funds tend to have very low expense ratios—by definition, they trade stocks rarely—but they have one great problem. Not only will they never beat the index they're meant to track, but they'll always underperform it slightly (the lag is due to the fund's expenses).

Insider buying   Legal purchases of stock by "insiders"—officers, directors, and anyone who owns 10% or more of the stock. Such trades, which must be reported to the Securities and Exchange

Commission, are an extremely positive sign. Insiders buy because they think the stock price will rise.

Insider selling   Legal sales of stock by "insiders" (see *Insider buying* above). Insider selling is not as accurate an indicator as an insider buying binge. People sell stock for many reasons—to buy a house or boat, pay tuition, or settle a divorce—but they buy for only one reason—income growth.

IPO   Short for initial public offering—the first time a company sells stock to the public. Also called *new issue*. IPOs often rise sharply right after the offering, only to fall back to earth six months or a year later.

Large-cap stock   See Small-cap stock.

Long-term debt   Debt that is due in a year or longer.

Market cap   Short for market capitalization. The market value of a public company, determined by multiplying the number of shares outstanding by the current stock price.

Micro-cap stock   See Small-cap stock.

Mid-cap stock   See Small-cap stock.

P/E ratio   Short for price/earnings ratio (or multiple). This is the price of the stock divided by its earnings for either the last full fiscal year of operations or—a better gauge—the latest twelve months of business. The ratio for *next* year's earnings is called the *estimated* or *projected* P/E.

PEG ratio   A terrific investment concept, this is the P/E ratio divided by the company's current or estimated growth rate. Ideally, you want to see a low P/E and a high growth rate, but life is seldom so accommodating. Second best is a P/E ratio that is much lower than the growth rate. When the PEG ratio is under .5, a stock is very attractive.

Pink Sheets   Where the fate of 3,000 nonlisted companies is tracked daily. The pages *are* pink, and the stocks are usually small—and rather illiquid. Don't mess with the Pink Sheets unless you've got a few years of investing under your belt. Two of the worst things about them: (1) it's often hard to get current quotes, and (2) the spread between the bid and asked prices sometimes verges on the astronomical. A stock might cost you $0.50 per share to buy but might fetch only $0.25 per share if you decide to sell it. With a spread like that, you're setting on a 50% loss the moment you buy—not counting commissions.

Preferred stock   The shares of stock you and I buy are almost exclusively "common" shares. Here's how the preference of preferred stocks works: If there is financial trouble, preferred shareholders receive all the dividends due them before common shareholders get any dividend payments. Preferred shareholders sometimes have an advantage as well when a company liquidates.

Preferred stock usually has a higher yield than common shares. That may be appealing to income-oriented investors, but it doesn't thrill me. Why? Because if a company does well, the total return achieved by the common stock will almost always exceed that of the preferred. I know it's common of me, but I'll take the higher returns.

Profit margin   This refers primarily to two important statistics, the *gross margin* and the *operating margin*. To arrive at the gross margin, subtract total costs from total revenue and then divide by total revenue. The operating margin is operating income divided by total revenue. A rising profit margin is a sign of corporate health; a declining one can be bad news.

Quick ratio   Similar to the current ratio, but more conservative because inventory is not counted as an asset. To calculate the ratio, divide total current assets (minus inventory) by total current liabilities. I want to see a quick ratio of 1 or higher.

Return on equity   A measurement of how well a company is using its capital to generate profits. Divide total earnings by total stockholders' equity to find the percentage result.

S&P 500   Short for the Standard & Poor's 500, an index of 500 of the largest publicly traded companies in the United States. The average person thinks of "the market" as the Dow Jones Industrial Average of 30 stocks. Most investment professionals, however, think of "the market" as the S&P 500. That's the benchmark many shoot to beat.

Selling short   Selling a stock that you don't actually own. You get the proceeds of the sale and then hope to buy back the shares—that is, "cover" your short position—when the price of the stock has fallen. The difference between the high price you sold at and the lower price you buy at is your profit.

Theoretically, at least. Short selling can be hazardous because many overvalued stocks get much more overvalued before they finally get chopped down to size.

Short-term debt   Debt that a company must repay within one year.

Small-cap stock   Unfortunately, the definitions of market professionals don't agree, but let's take a stab at it. Generally, small caps have market capitalizations of less than $250 million (some pros stretch the number to $500 million or more). Mid-caps range from $250 million to several billion. A large cap always has a valuation of more than $1 billion; usually, it's higher than $2 billion.

Standard & Poor's indexes of all three groups don't quite agree with the numbers above. The stocks in the S&P Small Cap 600 range in value from $96 million all the way up to $720 million. The S&P MidCap 400 starts at $300 million and goes as high as $5 billion. That ceiling is a bit strange because the median market cap of a stock in the S&P 500—the firm's large-cap index—is $4.7 billion. Translation: In the S&P universe, a small-cap can be larger than a mid-cap, and a mid-cap can be larger than a large-cap.

There's only one number professionals come even close to agreeing on. Micro-caps have market capitalizations of less than $100 million.

Stock screens   A sifting technique you can apply to all stocks, to find those that interest you. Investors commonly screen for low

P/E ratios, high dividends, high growth rates, and low PEG ratios. Many other criteria are also used.

Stop-loss order A stop-loss order is designed to limit your potential loss on any stock holding. At any time, you can tell your broker to place a stop-loss order on a stock you own. When it reaches that level, it will automatically be sold. Note: You don't always get the exit price you want. Say a company is trading at 36 and you have a stop order at 34. Then the company announces bad earnings. All trading is temporarily halted. The stock may reopen at 28, and your position is immediately liquidated at that price.

Total stockholders' equity The owners' equity in a corporation, derived from two key sources: (1) investments made by shareholders and (2) profits retained by the company.

Index

Index

Index

Index

Index

Index